THE Athenian Agora
Museum Guide

THE Athenian Agora

Museum Guide

FIFTH EDITION

Laura Gawlinski

with photographs by
Craig A. Mauzy

THE AMERICAN SCHOOL OF CLASSICAL STUDIES AT ATHENS
PRINCETON, NEW JERSEY

Book design and layout: Mary Jane Gavenda

Library of Congress Cataloging-in-Publication Data
Gawlinski, Laura.
  The Athenian Agora : museum guide / by Laura Gawlinski ; with photographs by Craig A. Mauzy.
—5th edition.
    pages cm
  Previous edition catalogued under title: Athenian Agora a guide to the excavation and museum
  Includes index.
  ISBN 978-0-87661-658-1 (alkaline paper)
  1. Museum of the Ancient Agora (Athens, Greece)—Guidebooks. 2. Agora (Athens, Greece)—
Guidebooks. 3. Archaeological museums and collections—Greece—Athens—Guidebooks. I. Title.
DF287.A23G39 2014
938'.5007449512—dc23   2013023944

Printed in Greece

Table of Contents

FOREWORD

THIS IS THE FIRST STAND-ALONE EDITION of the *Athenian Agora Museum Guide* and is intended as a companion to the fifth edition of the *Athenian Agora Site Guide* (J. McK. Camp II, 2010), which uses the icon **Ⓜ** to highlight objects in the museum. Further information about the antiquities and monuments of the site as well as a short history can be found there. Some material, particularly plans and images, has been repeated here in order to allow each guide to stand alone for convenient use by the visitor. Short bibliographic notes **▣** are at the end of most entries for the visitor who may wish to read more about artifacts on display.

Unless otherwise noted, all translations of inscriptions and texts are by Homer A. Thompson, Director of the Agora Excavations from 1947 until 1967.

Much of the material within this guidebook has been retained from the earlier editions of the *Agora Guide,* which combined into one volume the monuments on the site and the objects in the museum (see M. L. Lang and C. W. J. Eliot [1954], H. A. Thompson [1962, 1976], and J. McK. Camp II [1990]).

This guide takes account of the recent reorganization of the museum galleries, as well as new discoveries and recent scholarship. It is intended for visitors who are in Athens touring the site and is arranged following the order of display in the different areas of the Stoa of Attalos. A general plan of the site, with individual monuments numbered, is in a pocket in the back of the *Site Guide.* Monument numbers on the plan are cross-referenced in the text as **Ⓞ**. For accounts of the site that draw on the objects discovered there, see H. A. Thompson and R. E. Wycherley, *The Agora of Athens* (*Agora* XIV, 1972), and J. McK. Camp II, *The Athenian Agora* (London, 1986).

At the end of the book, the reader will find a list of the publications of the American School of Classical Studies at Athens that specifically concern material recovered from the Agora. Digital versions of a number of publications, and many other resources, are available through the Web site of the Agora excavations, http://www.ascsa.edu.gr/index.php/excavationagora.

This guide includes new color images, prepared by Craig A. Mauzy. Archival images were taken by a succession of Agora photographers: Alison Franz, James Heyle, Eugene Vanderpool Jr., Robert K. Vincent, and Craig A. Mauzy. Most of the drawings are the work of successive staff architects: John Travlos, William B. Dinsmoor Jr., and Richard Anderson. Support for the publication of the guidebook was provided in part by a grant from the Charles A. Dana Foundation.

Work in the Athenian Agora is sponsored by the American School of Classical Studies at Athens and the Packard Humanities Institute, with support from Randolph-Macon College, the Samuel H. Kress Foundation, and individual donors. The results described here were accomplished by hundreds of individuals. The views expressed are based on the combined thinking of the many scholars who have worked at the Agora excavations for over 80 years.

John McK. Camp II, Director, Agora Excavations

8

HISTORY AND TIMELINE

p. 102

p. 129

p. 41

p. 105

p. 156

p. 161

PREHISTORY AND PROTOHISTORY (3200–700 B.C.)	ARCHAIC PERIOD (700–480 B.C.)	CLASSICAL PERIOD (480–323 B.C.)

ca. 3200–2800 B.C.
Late Neolithic period.
Earliest recorded habitation in
Athens on the Acropolis slopes.

ca. 3000–1550 B.C.
**Early and Middle Helladic
periods.**

ca. 1550–1100 B.C.
**Mycenaean period (Late
Helladic or Late Bronze Age).**
Period of Greek mythology: fall
of Troy; Jason and the Argonauts;
Theseus and the Minotaur.

ca. 1100–700 B.C.
**Protogeometric and Geometric
periods (Early Iron Age).**
Period of Greek colonization/
migration; Olympic games start,
776 B.C.; introduction of the
alphabet; *Iliad* and *Odyssey*.

Late 7th century B.C.
Introduction of black-figure style of
painted pottery to Athens.

ca. 600 B.C.
Lawgiver Solon (594 B.C.),
beginnings of Athenian democracy.

560–510 B.C.
Rule of the tyrant Peisistratos and
his sons Hippias and Hipparchos.
Assassination of Hipparchos,
514 B.C.

ca. 515 B.C.
Red-figure style of painted pottery
appears in the Agora.

508/7 B.C.
Creation of Athenian democracy
under Kleisthenes.

490–479 B.C.
Persian Wars: Battles of Marathon
(490 B.C.), Thermopylai (480 B.C.),
Salamis (480 B.C.), and Plataia
(479 B.C.). Athens destroyed by
Persians, 480 B.C.

460–429 B.C.
Age of Perikles, rise of Athens.

431–404 B.C.
Peloponnesian War, Athens
versus Sparta (Peace of Nikias,
421–415 B.C.)

399 B.C.
Death of Sokrates.

338 B.C.
Rise of Macedon under Philip II and
Alexander; Battle of Chaironeia
(338 B.C.); Lykourgos in charge of
Athenian finances, 338–326 B.C.

323 B.C.
Death of Alexander the Great.

p. 64

p. 173

p. 55

p. 176

p. 181

p. 187

ELLENISTIC PERIOD (323–86 B.C.)	ROMAN PERIOD (86 B.C.–A.D. 250)	LATE ROMAN AND BYZANTINE (A.D. 250 +)

322 B.C.
Macedonian occupation of Athens begins.

Early 3rd century B.C.
Production of West Slope style of painted pottery begins.

ca. 225 B.C.
Production of moldmade bowls begins.

2nd century B.C.
Production of Neo-Attic sculpture begins.

159–138 B.C.
Building of the Stoa of Attalos, funded by Attalos II, king of Pergamon.

146 B.C.
Ascendancy of Rome in Greece. Sack of Corinth by Mummius.

86 B.C.
Siege and capture of Athens by the Roman general Sulla.

27 B.C.–A.D. 14
Reign of Augustus.

A.D. 117–138
Reign of Hadrian.

A.D. 138–161
Reign of Antoninus Pius.

ca. A.D. 150
Visit of Pausanias to Athens.

A.D. 267
Athens and the Agora burned by the Herulians.

A.D. 330
Founding of Constantinople.

A.D. 396
Invasion of Athens by Visigoths under Alaric; some damage to the Agora.

A.D. 529
Schools of Athens closed by the emperor Justinian.

A.D. 582/3
Devastation probably caused by Slavs; abandonment of the Agora.

10th–12th centuries A.D.
Reoccupation of Agora area; Church of the Holy Apostles built.

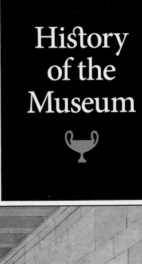

History of the Museum

Figure 1. Setting up Apollo Patroos in the reconstructed Stoa of Attalos (August 1956)

ALL OF THE FINDS FROM THE EXCAVATIONS conducted in the Agora by the American School of Classical Studies since 1931 are now housed in the Stoa of Attalos 46. Most of the outstanding pieces found in the course of the earlier Greek excavations have been transferred to the Stoa from the National Museum, among them the statues of Apollo Patroos (Fig. 1), a Corinthian capital from the Odeion of Agrippa (now on the site of the Odeion), and the personifications of the *Iliad* and the *Odyssey* (Fig. 25; p. 37). The material from the excavations carried out by the American School on the north slope of the Acropolis and on the Pnyx is also deposited in the Stoa.

The history of the museum is intertwined with the history of the reconstruction of the Stoa of Attalos. Within a few years of the beginning of the excavations at the Agora, the Old Excavation House was no longer sufficient (Fig. 2), and plans for an on-site museum to present the objects in their context were well underway even before the outbreak of World War II. The area west of the Areopagus 74 seemed a suitable location for such a museum, and in 1946, preliminary excavations began there and sketches of potential building plans were drawn up. When the excavations brought to light an unanticipated number of important features and finds, excavation director Homer A. Thompson recommended restoration of an ancient building as a solution to the problem of location. The Stoa of Attalos (built by King Attalos II of Pergamon, 159–138 B.C.) was chosen because the building form was suitable for museum galleries and workspace, and enough of the original structure was preserved to permit accurate restoration. The north end even stood to the original roof line. The reconstruction was carried out with the generous financial support of John D. Rockefeller Jr. between 1953–1956 (Fig. 3). In June 1957 the Greek Archaeological Service assumed responsibility for maintaining and guarding the archaeological

Figure 2. Courtyard of the old excavation house

Figure 3. The Stoa of Attalos after reconstruction (1956)

area and the Stoa of Attalos. In preparation for the 2004 Olympics, the Hellenic Ministry of Culture cleaned the façade of the Stoa of Attalos and the ground floor colonnade and reorganized and reno- vated the galleries of the museum. In 2012 a new exhibition on the upper floor was opened to the public made possible by funding from the European Economic Area (EEA) and the Hellenic Ministry of Development, Competitiveness, and Shipping.

Today, the Stoa not only provides ample space for storage, research, and the display of objects, but also allows the visitor to appreciate the function and form of this common type of ancient public building. It is an excellent example of the fully developed type of stoa: on each of its two stories a two-aisled colonnade was backed by a row of 21 rooms, which served chiefly as shops. In front, a broad terrace ran the entire length of the building. The chief function of the Stoa was to provide a sheltered promenade for informal interaction, which must also have assured its success as a shopping center. The shops were rented by the state to individual merchants, so the build- ing would have served as a source of revenue as well as an ornament to the city. Note the adaptation of the lower, Doric order for a stoa, a building designed for use by numerous people, unlike a temple. These

Doric columns are more widely spaced for easy access, and the lower third of each exterior column is left unfluted so as to prevent damage by people and goods passing in and out of the colonnade.

After undergoing various slight alterations in the course of four centuries, the Stoa shared in the destruction of A.D. 267 by the Herulians, a Germanic tribe. Note the effects of fire on the inner face of the south end wall. A few years later it was incorporated into the Post-Herulian Wall, at which time the facade and all the columns were dismantled for use in strengthening the rear part of the building. The back rooms continued to be used into Ottoman times (15th century).

The survival of enough of the walls and architectural members made possible a detailed and certain restoration. Specimens of the various ancient members were added into the reconstruction, especially toward the south end of the building near the entrance. The restoration was carried out in the same materials as the original: marble for the facade, columns, and interior trim; limestone for the walls; and terracotta tiles for the roof. The upper floor and the roof are now supported on beams of reinforced concrete enclosed in wooden shells that reproduce exactly the spacing and dimensions of the original beams of solid wood. The design of the wooden doors was recovered from cuttings in the marble jambs and thresholds, and from the analogy of surviving ancient tomb doors made of marble in imitation of wood.

Through this reconstruction, the visitor can understand the suitability of stoas as public gathering spaces. The spacious colonnades provided shelter for literally thousands of people, protecting them from sun in summer and wind and rain in winter, while allowing light and fresh air in abundance.

Agora XIV (1972), pp. 230–233; C. A. Mauzy, *Agora Excavations, 1931–2006: A Pictorial History* (Athens, 2006), pp. 26–73.

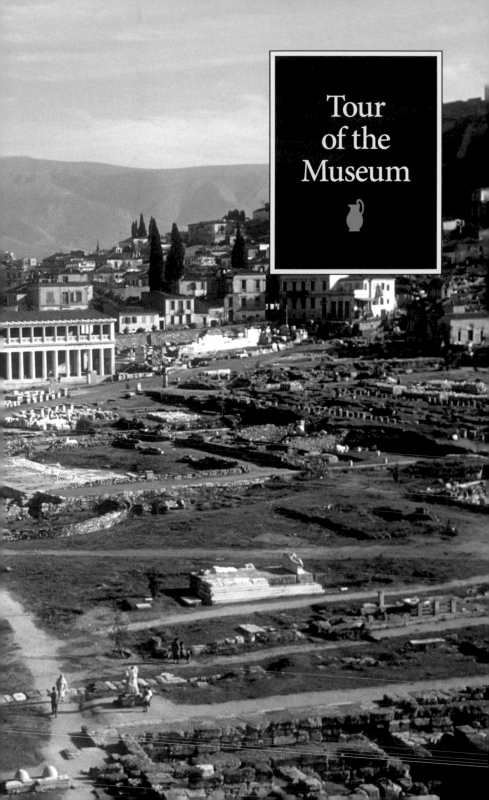

Tour of the Museum

LAYOUT OF THE MUSEUM

The following parts of the building are usually open to the public (Fig. 4a–c):

- Terrace: various marbles, chiefly architectural
- Ground floor, colonnade: sculpture and inscriptions
- Ground floor, area of shops: museum gallery, sales room
- Upper floor: sculpture and models of the ancient city

ℹ️ Entry to the museum is included in the Agora admission fee.

📷 Handheld photography is permitted without flash.

❗ Guests are kindly reminded not to touch or sit on the antiquities.

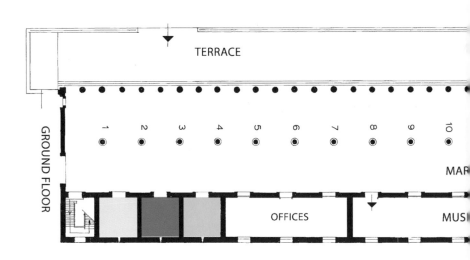

Figure 4a. Stoa of Attalos, plan of the ground floor

The museum offices and workrooms are installed in the area of the ancient shops on the upper floor. The greater part of the archaeological material is shelved on the upper floor behind a frosted glass screen and in magazines in the basement. A few of the screen's panes are transparent, and allow visitors to view original wooden cases containing artifacts from the excavations. Students may be admitted to the workrooms and magazine on application at the museum offices.

Wheelchair access is at the north. Washrooms and a drinking fountain are on the ground floor, north end.

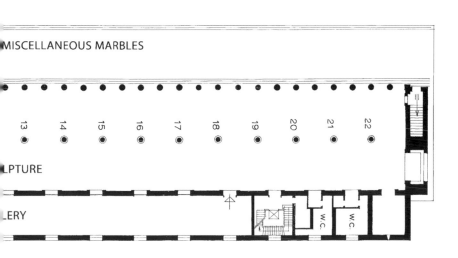

MEMORIAL ROOM
SALES INFORMATION
WINE JARS

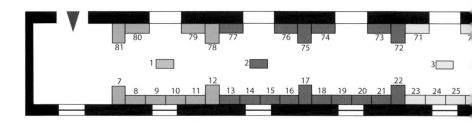

Figure 4b. Stoa of Attalos, plan of the museum: detail of museum gallery with cases color-coded by time period.

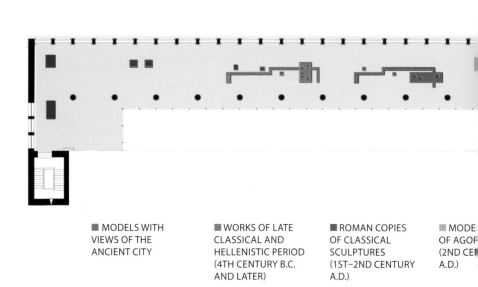

■ MODELS WITH VIEWS OF THE ANCIENT CITY

■ WORKS OF LATE CLASSICAL AND HELLENISTIC PERIOD (4TH CENTURY B.C. AND LATER)

■ ROMAN COPIES OF CLASSICAL SCULPTURES (1ST–2ND CENTURY A.D.)

■ MODE OF AGOF (2ND CE A.D.)

Fig. 4c. Upper floor: sculpture and models of the ancient city.

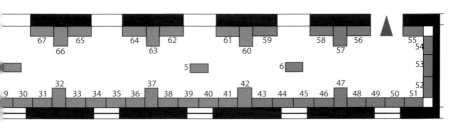

■ PREHISTORIC   ■ EARLY IRON AGE   ■ ARCHAIC   ■ CLASSICAL   ■ HELLENISTIC, ROMAN,
AND BYZANTINE

OMAN RTRAITS T−2ND TURY A.D.)	■ HERMS WITH PORTRAITS OF STATE OFFICIALS (2ND−3RD CENTURY A.D.)	■ ROMAN PORTRAITS (3RD CENTURY A.D.)	■ PLAN OF AGORA (5TH CENTURY A.D.)	■ COLLECTION OF SCULPTURES ADORNING THE PRIVATE SCHOOLS OF LATE ANTIQUITY

TERRACE

🔁 Entrance at the south

Miscellaneous marbles from all parts of the excavation are assembled here; the range of objects provides an instructive overview both of architectural fragments and of the sorts of monuments that were once set up in or near the Agora.

Summer visitors can cool off at the small fountain at the south end of the terrace. This fountain was built in place of a much larger one contemporary with the Stoa. As indicated by the *stele* (upright stone slab), the bench and restored fountain together form a memorial to Theodore Leslie Shear, field director of the Agora excavations from their inception in 1931 until his death in 1945. Beside this fountain is a rectangular marble altar dedicated to Artemis (Fig. 5; I 7635). The

images carved onto the sides of the altar depict satyrs and maenads sacrificing animals; these figures are associated with Dionysos rather than Artemis, and their presence reflects the altar's findspot in a building used for the worship of Dionysos in the valley just west of the Agora. This is the first of many altars on display, which together serve to illustrate the variety of shapes, materials, and deities in whose worship they were used.

To the right of this altar stands a statue base signed by Theoxenos the Theban (Fig. 6; I 5407). This marble pedestal once carried portrait statues of a man and his wife—Physteus and Peisikrateia of Acharnai. These statues were dedicated by their son, Demopeithides, to Demeter and Kore. The work

Figure 5. Altar of Artemis

Figure 6. Statue base of Theoxenos

is signed in smaller lettering below the dedication by the otherwise unknown artist, Theoxenos the Theban. The statue base dates to the second half of the 4th century B.C. The two blocks of Demopeithides' monument were found in the Eleusinion ⑤⑥ where the group likely stood. Peisikrateia is perhaps to be identified as the figure opposite Column 4 (p. 40, S 1016).

The final object of note at the south end of the terrace is a *perirrhanterion,* a water basin used for purification (Fig. 7; A 2115). A similar basin can be seen on site near the boundary stones ⑩.

To the north, on the other side of the terrace entrance, is a battered statue of the Mother of the Gods in her typical seated form (Fig. 8; S 1356). The Mother's sanctuary in the Agora was the Metroon ⑭, and another of her images is on display in the museum gallery in Case 59 (p. 172). Next, compare two of the statue bases nearby (Fig. 9): I 6532 bears foot-shaped cuttings, indicating it was a base for a bronze statue, while

Figure 7. A perirrhanterion

*Figure 8. Statue of the
Mother of the Gods to
the left of the terrace
entrance*

Figure 9. Statue bases I 6532 (top) and I 5484 (bottom)

the large rectangular cutting of the nearby I 5484 (= *IG* I³ 953) is suitable for a monument of a different sort, probably a large pillar to carry the dedicatory wreaths mentioned in the inscription on its front face.

Funerary monuments are also well represented on the terrace. To the right, the base of the Roman period featuring inscriptions in both Latin and Greek (Fig. 10; I 774) is significant as one of only a handful of Latin inscriptions found in the Agora.

Not far from the bilingual funerary monument is an altar for Zeus Phratrios and Athena Phratria (Fig. 11; I 6709, cf. I 3706 on site ㉔).

Figure 10. Bilingual (Latin and Greek) funerary monument

It still retains some of the metal in the clamp cuttings that once held the four-sided marble structure together.

Figure 11. Altar for Zeus Phratrios and Athena Phratria

Figure 12. Poros offering table from the area of the Eleusinion

Many other architectural fragments follow. At roughly the middle of the terrace is an offering table, carved from poros (soft limestone), from the vicinity of the Eleusinion **56** (Fig. 12; A 2890). Nearby is a roughly worked, inscribed stone that once marked land that was mortgaged as part of a dowry pledge (Fig. 13; I 7001).

Further north are funerary monuments of various shapes. Three figures are carved on the fragmentary marble *lekythos* of the 4th century B.C. (Fig. 14; I 5459). An inscription above the head of the seated man informs us that his name was Timokrates; the inscriptions that once labeled the others are no longer readable. The gesture of clasped right hands—called *dexiosis*—is a typical funerary motif that illustrates the communion between the deceased (in this case the seated man) and the family. Further on is a *stele* with a palmette (Fig. 15; I 4970). This simple marker is next to the first of two sarcophagi on the terrace, a very fine example of the late Archaic period (ca. 520–480 B.C.) likely from an early cemetery southwest of the public square **74** (Fig. 16; A 1129).

Figure 13. Mortgage inscription

Figure 14 (left). Fragmentary marble grave marker in the shape of a lekythos

Figure 15 (right). Sepulchral stele *with palmette*

Figure 16. Marble sarcophagus of the Archaic period

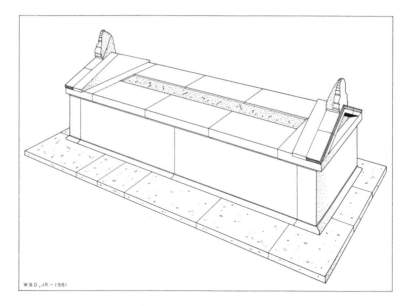

W.B.D., JR.—1981

Figure 17. Restored view of the Altar of Aphrodite

In this area, one can also examine the decorative altar fragments (A 3774 a and b) almost certainly associated with the altar of Aphrodite Ourania **36** (Fig. 17). A series of poros altars (A 774, A 775, A 2827, and A 2828) from the vicinity of the Eleusinion **56** are set up here as well (Fig. 18).

At the north end of the terrace rest a few marble puteals (well covers), most with obvious rope wear (e.g., Fig. 19; A 1085), and a second sarcophagus now used as a planter (A 2519).

Occasionally new pieces are added and others returned to the site or taken for conservation. For example, the bathtub (Fig. 20; ST 334) possibly associated with the circular bathhouse **73** is now to be found in a marble pile directly south of the monopteros **43** outside the Stoa amid some trees.

Statue base of Theoxenos: B. D. Meritt, *Hesperia* 26 (1957), pp. 203–206, no. 51; *Agora* III (1957; reprinted 1973), p. 83, no. 228; *Agora* XIV (1972), pp. 153–154; *Agora* XXXI (1998), pp. 189–190, no. 11. **Bilingual monument:** *Agora* XXXV (2013), pp. 220–221, no. 385. **Marble lekythos:** *Agora* XXXV (2013), p. 147, no. 182. **Palmette stele:** *Agora* XXXV (2013), pp. 133–134, no. 153.

Figure 18 (top). Poros altars from the area of the Eleusinion

Figure 19 (left). Marble puteal with rope wear

Figure 20 (bottom). Stone bathtub possibly from the bathhouse at the southeast of the Agora square

WORKING WITH MARBLE

The terrace and colonnade are filled with marble objects: sculpture, bases for monuments or statues, inscriptions, and building fragments. There were a variety of sources for this marble, both local and foreign. The two most important local sources were the mountains Pentelikon (to the northeast) and Hymettos (to the southeast); the former produced a fine-grained white marble (Pentelic); the latter, typically a pale bluish-gray one (Hymettian). For finer sculpture, often a coarser-grained marble imported from the island of Paros was preferred. This variation is seen on the Hephaisteion ❶, where the building above foundation level is Pentelic, but the sculpted metopes—the rectangular slabs of the frieze running above the columns—are Parian. However, the widespread importation of marble from outside Attica did not become popular until the Romans gained control of the quarries throughout their empire. In the Agora, the facade of the stage from the Odeion of Agrippa ㊶ (Fig. 21; A 1174, p. 40) illustrates how different marble types were combined in this period: the greenish marble slabs are Karystian, from a quarry in Euboia; their color is juxtaposed with the white

Figure 21. Colored marble used in the stage facade from the Odeion

Figure 22. Modern marbleworker at work on the reconstruction of the Stoa of Attalos using replicas of ancient tools

Pentelic Herms and lotus-palmette pattern, set on top of a plinth of bluish Hymettian.

Along the edges of the public square of the Agora were several workshops where, after some preliminary shaping in the quarries, the production of various marble pieces would have been completed. Excavation of the House of Mikion and Menon ⓱ (5th–3rd centuries B.C.) and the Roman workshops in the area of the Library of Pantainos ㊽ have revealed fragments of the iron tools used by sculptors. Hammers, chisels, and drills were used to increase the fineness of the surface in stages; the final, smallest toolmarks could then be removed with emery or pumice (Fig. 22). Toolmarks of different sizes and types can still be seen on unfinished pieces and those objects that were not meant to be viewed from every angle. Backsides and sections set into bases or the ground often were left rougher.

After carving was complete, the object could be smoothed and then polished with wax or olive oil. A few sculptures in the museum gallery preserve the paint that would have been applied next (Aphrodite, S 1192, p. 172; satyr, S 221, p. 173). Final touches might include the addition of details in stone or metal: eyes, eyelashes, wreaths, or spears like those of the horsemen on the cavalry victory relief (Fig. 28; I 7167, pp. 46–48).

Many people must have been employed in Athens in the business of working marble and other stone, especially during great building projects as under Perikles. For carving the pediment of the Parthenon in 434/3 B.C., the city paid the sculptors 16,392 drachmas (*IG* I³ 449; a day's wage was about 1 drachma at the time). Famous sculptors at the Agora include Praxiteles (statue base I 4165, p. 33, is signed by him). The father of Sokrates was also a marbleworker, and perhaps the philosopher briefly followed in his footsteps.

Bronze was preferred for freestanding sculpture in the Classical period, but in the Roman period the demand for Greek art led to a sharp increase in marble copies. A cast of the original could be made for transferring measurements to stone, but sometimes the process must have been more freehand. Because the majority of those Classical bronze statues are gone—carted off by invaders or melted down for their precious metal—the marble copies are very important today, especially when they can be identified with artworks known otherwise only from literature. Case 59 in the museum gallery (p. 172) and the upper floor contain several such examples.

In addition to sculpture and architecture, marble was a common medium for the inscription and public presentation of laws and decrees. Although no names of inscribers have come down to us, it is often possible to identify "handwriting" and determine if several inscriptions were carved by the same person. Sculpture, architectural elements, and text could also be combined, as is the case with record reliefs like the law on tyranny (Fig. 77; I 6524, pp. 151–152).

AgPicBk 27 (2006); O. Palagia, ed. *Greek Sculpture: Function, Materials, and Techniques in the Archaic and Classical Periods* (Cambridge, 2006); A. Stewart, *Hesperia* 82 (2013), pp. 615–650.

GROUND FLOOR: COLONNADE

 One may find it best to stroll the colonnade in a counter-clockwise direction, which returns the visitor to the entrance into the museum gallery and the staircase to the upper floor, both at the south end. The guide follows this route, describing first the objects along the shop entrances and then returning down the central colonnade, diverting from this path when objects across from one another are best viewed together.

CULT STATUE OF APOLLO PATROOS

To the right, as one enters the colonnade of the building, against the ancient south wall, stands a colossal statue of Apollo in Pentelic marble (Fig. 23; S 2154: 4th century B.C.). The head was inset and is missing; the arms are broken away. Against his left side, the god once held a *kithara* (a handheld stringed instrument used by professional musicians), and he wears the heavy formal dress (*peplos* and *himation*) customary for him as god of music. A miniature ancient copy of the statue is exhibited in Case 59 in the museum gallery (S 877, p. 172). The statue was found in 1907 by Greek excavators on the west side of the Agora. It has been recognized as the cult statue from the Temple of Apollo Patroos ㉓, a work attributed by Pausanias (1.3.4) to the artist Euphranor, one of the leading sculptors and painters at Athens in the middle of the 4th century B.C.

H. A. Thompson, *ArchEph* 1953–1954 Γ΄ (1961), pp. 30–44; S. Adam, *The Technique of Greek Sculpture in the Archaic and Classical Periods* (Oxford, 1966), pp. 94–97; J. Travlos, *Pictorial Dictionary of Ancient Athens* (London, 1971), pp. 96–97; *Agora* XIV (1972), p. 139; O. Palagia, *Euphranor* (Leiden, 1980), pp. 13–20; C. Hedrick, *AJA* 92 (1988), pp. 198–200; *AgPicBk* 27 (2006), pp. 40–41; M. Lawall, *Hesperia* 78 (2009), pp. 396–401.

STATUE BASE SIGNED BY PRAXITELES

The pedestal of white marble (I 4165: 4th century B.C.) to the left of Apollo carried two statues, portraits of Spoudias and his wife Kleiokrateia. The statues were dedicated to Demeter and Kore. The couple is also known from the forty-first oration of Demosthenes, where they are cited as participants in an unseemly family quarrel. In modest lettering below the name of Kleiokrateia on the right side of the front of the base appears the signature of the most famous Athenian sculptor of the 4th century B.C.: Praxiteles. On the fragmentary left side of the front are scattered letters from the names of Spoudias and of another sculptor who did his portrait. The base was found to the north of the

Hephaisteion in a foundation of the Early Roman period. It had probably stood in a sanctuary of Demeter seen by Pausanias (1.2.4) inside the Dipylon ㉙, where it must have suffered in the Roman siege of 86 B.C.

T. L. Shear, *Hesperia* 6 (1937), pp. 339–342; B. D. Meritt, *Hesperia* 26 (1957), pp. 200–203, no. 50; J. Marcadé, *Recueil des signatures des sculpteurs grecs* 2 (Paris, 1957), no. 115; *Agora* III (1957; reprinted 1973), p. 85, no. 228; *AgPicBk* 10 (1966), fig. 27; *Agora* XIV (1972), pp. 154–155; *Agora* XXXI (1998), pp. 188–189, no. 7.

IONIC COLUMN CAPITAL AND BASE FROM THE STOA OF ATTALOS

Across from the statue base, beside Interior Column 1, are one of the original bases (A 2567: 2nd century B.C.) for the series of columns in the interior of the Stoa—found in its original position but moved for preservation—and a capital (A 2073: 2nd century B.C.) assembled from many fragments of the original. These members served as the basis for the restoration.

J. Travlos, *Pictorial Dictionary of Ancient Athens* (London, 1971), fig. 651; A. Paterakis, *OSGP* 5 (1997), p. 79.

IONIC COLUMN CAPITAL WITH PAINTED DECORATION

An Ionic capital of Pentelic marble (A 2973: 5th century B.C.) stands against the wall between the doors of what were once Shops A and B (Fig. 24). This capital was extracted from the Post-Herulian Wall to the south of the Stoa of Attalos ㊾. With it were found the complete column now standing in Shop A (A 2972, p. 72) and two shafts from the same series now lying in front of the Library of Pantainos (see p. 136 of the *Agora Site Guide*). All come from an otherwise unknown building of the third quarter of the 5th century B.C. Masons' marks show that they had served some intermediate use before being incorporated into the Post-Herulian Wall in the 3rd century A.D. One can still see (but please do not touch) traces of the ancient paint used

Figure 23 (at left). Apollo Patroos(?), perhaps by Euphranor, second half of the 4th century B.C.

Figure 24. Ionic capital of the third quarter of the 5th century B.C. with watercolor showing its polychromy

to emphasize the carved details. Compare to the later Attalid capital (A 2073, above) to see the changes in the Ionic order over time.

H. A. Thompson, *Hesperia* 29 (1960), pp. 351–356; J. Travlos *Pictorial Dictionary of Ancient Athens* (London, 1971), fig. 153; *Agora* XIV (1972), p. 166; L. S. Meritt, *Hesperia* 65 (1996), pp. 129–130, 154–156, no. 14B.

PERSONIFICATIONS OF THE *ILIAD* AND *ODYSSEY* WITH INSCRIBED BASE

The robust female figures in armor (S 2038, S 2039, I 6628: 2nd century A.D.) opposite Column 2 are personifications of the *Iliad* and the *Odyssey*. The clue to the identification was given by the combination of figures on the armor of the smaller statue (Fig. 25). Monstrous Skylla, with dogs extending from her lower body, occupies the cuirass. On the upper lappets are shown Aiolos, god of the winds; three bird-winged sirens playing musical instruments; and the cyclops Polyphemos, represented with a third eye on his forehead. All these recall scenes of the *Odyssey*. On one of the long lower lappets of this figure is the

Figure 25. Cuirass of the personification of the Odyssey, *2nd century* A.D.

signature of the artist: Jason the Athenian. Traces of a sword on the right side of the companion figure are appropriate to the *Iliad*, who is also marked as the older sister by her larger size and greater maturity. The identification was confirmed by the discovery of the plinth of the *Iliad*, now displayed to the right of the statue. The plinth, which was cut from the same block of Pentelic marble as the statue, is inscribed with an epigram:

> *The Iliad, I that was after Homer and before Homer, have*
> *been set up alongside him who bore me in his youth.*

In the same context as the plinth was found the left leg of the *Iliad* (not exhibited). Based on the epigram, the group may be restored with a figure of Homer, perhaps seated, flanked to right and left by the personifications of his two great works, like a father with his daughters.

The statues came to light in 1869 at the southwest corner of the Stoa of Attalos; the inscribed base and the leg were recovered from a nearby Byzantine wall in 1953. Provenance, date (early 2nd century A.D.), and theme would all be appropriate for the association of the group with the Library of Pantainos **48**. As yet, however, no suitable base has been found in the Library.

G. Treu, *AM* 14 (1889), pp. 160–169; H. A. Thompson, *Hesperia* 23 (1954), pp. 62–65; A. E. Raubitscheck, *Hesperia* 23 (1954), pp. 317–319; *Agora* III (1957; reprinted 1973), no. 464; G. M. Richter, *The Portraits of the Greeks* 1 (London, 1965), pp. 53–54; J. Travlos, *Pictorial Dictionary of Ancient Athens* (1971), pp. 233–234; *Agora* XIV (1972), p. 115; K. Seaman in *Personification in the Greek World: From Antiquity to Byzantium* (Aldershot, 2005), pp. 173–189.

STATUE OF A GODDESS, PROBABLY APHRODITE HEGEMONE

The imperious female figure (S 378: ca. 170–150 B.C.) opposite Column 3, of well over life size and of Pentelic marble, was found in the Post-Herulian Wall ❹ in the area of the Library of Pantainos (Fig. 26). Head, right arm, and right foot were all attached separately and are now missing. Above a tightly fitted *chiton* the goddess wears a mantle that is draped precariously over the left shoulder and the right thigh. The left hand rests with outspread fingers on the hip. The right arm was raised high as though to grasp a scepter or the like.

This sculptural type was widespread in the Hellenistic world, and the statue from the Agora is one of the most monumental examples of its use. The type was employed for various divinities, certainly for Artemis, but also for Aphrodite as illustrated by a miniature example from the Agora (S 1192, Case 59, p. 172). It has been argued, therefore, that the original location of this Aphrodite was outside the northwest corner of the Agora in the sanctuary to Aphrodite Hegemone, Demos, and the Graces ❸.

It may also be noted that the statue was found in the Post-Herulian Wall close to the Aphrodite described below (S 1882, p. 41), and in close association with elements from the ceiling of the Temple of Ares ❸. It is likely, therefore, that these are the two Aphrodites seen by Pausanias (1.8.4) in the Temple of Ares. Aphrodite Hegemone would have been moved into the Ares temple from her original cult spot before Pausanias visited in the 2nd century A.D.

T. L. Shear, *Hesperia* 4 (1935), pp. 384–386; E. B. Harrison, *Hesperia* 29 (1960), p. 374; E. B. Harrison in *Akten des XIII. Internationalen Kongresses für klassische Archäologie, Berlin 1988* (Mainz, 1990), p. 346; O. Palagia in *The Archaeology of Athens and Attica under the Democracy* (Oxford, 1994), pp. 115, 120; A. Stewart, *Hesperia* 81 (2012), pp. 288–289, 311, 318–319.

Figure 26 (at right). Aphrodite Hegemone(?), ca. 170–150 B.C.

STATUE OF A WOMAN

The much-battered statue in Pentelic marble of a woman of mature years (S 1016: mid-4th century B.C.) opposite Column 4, heavily draped in *chiton* and *himation*, is of a type appropriate to the middle of the 4th century B.C. The statue was found just to the west of the Eleusinion 56, where it probably stood. The figure may be Peisikrateia from the pedestal that was once in the Eleusinion and is now on the terrace of the Stoa (I 5407, p. 23).

HERMS USED AS SUPPORTING FIGURES

The female portrait is flanked to right and left by Herms (S 33: 2nd century A.D.; S 198: Roman), representations of the god Hermes in the form of a four-sided post with an anthropomorphized head and phallus. Both of the Herms on display once served as supports at the sides of major statues. That on the right, in which the god is bearded, bore the weight of a child in a group comparable with the Hermes and Dionysos at Olympia. It may even be a copy of a bronze group of the two gods by Kephisodotos the Elder, as described by Pliny the Elder (34.87). The other figure represents the youthful, beardless Hermes; he retains over his head the bunched cloak of the larger figure that stood beside the Herm. Both figures were found on the west side of the Agora.

Agora XI (1965), nos. 210–213; A. Corso, *The Art of Praxiteles: The Development of Praxiteles' Workshop and its Cultural Tradition Until the Sculptor's Acme (364–1 B.C.)* (Rome, 2004), pp. 77–85; C. A. Mauzy, *Agora Excavations, 1931–2006: A Pictorial History* (Athens, 2006), pp. 18–19.

ODEION OF AGRIPPA, PARTS OF THE STAGE FRONT AND HEAD OF A TRITON

Opposite Column 5 are eight objects from the Odeion of Agrippa 41 (A 1174 + A 586 + S 553 + S 554 + S 558 + S 1391 + S 1213: ca. 15 B.C.; S 1214: ca. A.D. 150). The restoration of the section of the stage front is based on ancient fragments found in the ruins of the building (Fig. 21). The front was paneled with slabs of greenish marble from Karystos in Euboia set between Herms carved in local white Pentelic marble; it was supported on a plinth of bluish Hymettian marble, also local, and surmounted by a crowning member in white marble delicately carved with interlacing lotus and palmette. Male and female heads were used, presumably in alternation. Both the heads and the carved ornament of the crowning member are good examples of the classicizing work of the Augustan period (ca. 15 B.C.).

The head of a Triton on the wall above the stage front comes from one of six colossal figures—three Tritons and three Giants—carved ca. A.D. 150 to adorn the facade of the Odeion of Agrippa. The Tritons have been shown to be adaptations of the Poseidon of the west pediment of the Parthenon; as such they illustrate the classicizing tendency of the Antonine period. This head was discovered at Eleusis (some 14 miles away!), but the neck that joins the head was found in front of the Odeion.

General: H. A. Thompson, *Hesperia* 19 (1950), pp. 64–68, 106; J. Travlos, *Pictorial Dictionary of Ancient Athens* (London, 1971), pp. 365–366, figs. 485–487; *Agora* XIV (1972), p. 113. **Stage**: A. Paterakis, *OSGP* 5 (1997), p. 80. **Triton**: O. Palagia, *The Pediments of the Parthenon* (Leiden, 1993), pp. 9, 47.

STATUE OF A GODDESS, PROBABLY APHRODITE

The headless statue of a goddess of slightly more than life size (S 1882: ca. 420 B.C.) opposite Column 6 has been reassembled from scores of fragments of Parian marble found in the Post-Herulian Wall ㊾ near the southwest corner of the Library of Pantainos (photo p. 10, top right). In its flamboyance of figure and drapery combined with great delicacy of execution the statue recalls the parapet of the Nike Temple on the Athenian Acropolis and the vase paintings of the Meidias Painter. These comparisons suggest a date of ca. 420 B.C. The statue represents a goddess surely; Aphrodite almost certainly. Since many fragments from the marble ceiling of the Temple of Ares were found together with the statue, this may be one of the two Aphrodites noted by Pausanias (1.8.4) in the sanctuary of Ares ㊳. See also S 378, p. 38.

E. B. Harrison, *Hesperia* 29 (1960), pp. 373–376; S. Adam, *The Technique of Greek Sculpture in the Archaic and Classical Periods* (Oxford, 1966), pp. 16, 52–53; O. Palagia in *The Archaeology of Athens and Attica under the Democracy* (Oxford, 1994), p. 115; A. Stewart, *Hesperia* 81 (2012), p. 276.

STATUE OF A WOMAN, POSSIBLY APHRODITE

Past the entrance of the museum gallery, opposite Columns 8 and 9, stands the lower part of a female figure in Pentelic marble, clad in a very thin dress with a cloak hunched in front of the right thigh and draped over the extended left arm (S 37: ca. 400–380 B.C.). Much of the front drapery was worked in a separate piece and inset, in consequence of some flaw that appeared in the marble as it was being carved. On top of the drapery over the left arm is the curved bedding for another patch. The back is unfinished. The style of the drapery and the high quality of the workmanship point to a date in the first quarter of the 4th century B.C. The statue had been built into a late foundation at the southeast corner of the Metroon ⓮, and its freshness suggests that it stood somewhere in that area in a sheltered position. An identification as Aphrodite is suggested by stylistic similarities to other sculptures of the goddess.

T. L. Shear, *Hesperia* 2 (1933), pp. 175–178; B. Schlörb, *Untersuchungen zur Bildhauergeneration nach Phidias* (Waldsassen, 1964), p. 53; S. Adam, *The Technique of Greek Sculpture in the Archaic and Classical Periods* (Oxford, 1966), pp. 15, 20, 31, 34; A. Stewart, *Hesperia* 81 (2012), pp. 277–278.

TORSO OF A WOMAN, POSSIBLY APHRODITE

Move along to the column opposite—Column 9—instead of continuing along the wall. Here is the upper part of a female figure of Pentelic marble (S 210: ca. 400 B.C.), which must have come from a statue with drapery like that of the previous figure, and of equally fine workmanship. The now-missing head was carved separately. This figure, too, might be Aphrodite.

A. Stewart, *Hesperia* 81 (2012), p. 277.

TWO STATUES OF GODDESSES

The two draped female figures of Pentelic marble (S 462, S 473: ca. 150–86 B.C.) against the wall opposite Columns 9 and 10 were found together with several more fragmentary statues built into a screen wall of the Early Roman period around the little square to the south of the New Bouleuterion ⓭. There is good reason to regard them as victims of the Sullan siege of 86 B.C., which provides a convenient lower terminus for their date. The head of S 462 on the left was inset; that of S 473 on the right was cut in one piece with the torso. Both may be taken as characteristic Athenian products of the Hellenistic period. Each wears a tightly fitted *chiton* and a voluminous *himation*. Each is girt with a cord that encircles the chest below the breasts and is then carried over the shoulders. The remnants of Eros on the left shoulder of S 473 mark her as Aphrodite. She rests her left arm on a tree trunk, a motif likely inspired by the famous cult statue of "Aphrodite in the Gardens" of the late 5th century B.C. by Alkamenes (described by Pausanias, 1.19.2). Her figure also blends features from the Pheidian Ourania type, perhaps suggesting that she once stood as a dedication in the sanctuary of Aphrodite Ourania ❸❻. S 462 retains no attribute. She gives the impression of a dancing figure, perhaps a Nymph or Grace, but is even more likely to be yet another Aphrodite.

General: H. A. Thompson, *Hesperia* 6 (1937), p. 168. **S 462**: A. Stewart, *Hesperia* 81 (2012), pp. 298–310, 320. **S 473**: A. Delivorrias, *AntP* 8.3 (1968), p. 26; A. Stewart, *Hesperia* 81 (2012), pp. 298–310, 321–322.

VOTIVE RELIEF DEDICATED TO PAN AND THE NYMPHS

Between the statues of goddesses opposite Columns 9 and 10 is a Pentelic marble relief in which a number of divinities are gathered in a cave marked as a sanctuary by a rustic altar near its middle (Fig. 27; I 7154: ca. 330 B.C.). From left to right the figures may be recognized as Demeter, Apollo (seated), Artemis, Hermes, three Nymphs (one seated), Pan (seated on the rock filling his mug from a wine skin), and the horned river god Achelous, of whom only traces remain at the extreme right. Above reclines Zeus, who looks attentively at what is taking place near the altar. Pan, Achelous, and the Nymphs are constant companions, and are commonly found together in cave sanctuaries. The relief was probably dedicated in the well-known cave of Pan on the northwest shoulder of the Acropolis. Apollo and Demeter (and likely Zeus) also had shrines on the north slope of the Acropolis, so the scene represents a neighborly gathering.

There are two different interpretations of the central scene that have brought these gods together. It might depict Hermes delivering the infant Dionysos, newly born from the thigh of Zeus, into the hands of one of the Nymphs who will see to the young god's upbringing.

THE ATHENIAN AGORA: MUSEUM GUIDE

Figure 27. Votive relief of the Cave of Pan, second half of the 4th century B.C.

But it can also be read as the story of another baby, Ion, the mythical founder of the Ionian people, through whom the Athenians traced their ancestry. Because Ion was abandoned on the north slope of the Acropolis, this interpretation links the subject of the relief to the place where it was likely dedicated.

The interest of the relief is enhanced by the name of the dedicator that appears on the base in front: Neoptolemos, son of Antikles, of the deme (township) of Melite. This man is known to have been a very wealthy citizen in the second half of the 4th century B.C. who was commended repeatedly for his civic and religious benefactions. A date of ca. 330 B.C. would suit the known career of the dedicator and the style of the relief.

The relief was found lying face down in the peristyle of the Omega House **58**. The heads of all the figures have been deliberately mutilated, likely out of Christian zeal, and the key figure, the infant, has suffered most grievously.

T. L. Shear Jr., *Hesperia* 42 (1973), pp. 168–170; T. L. Shear Jr., *OpRom* 9 (1973), pp. 183–191; H. A. Thompson, *JWalt* 36 (1977), pp. 73–84; A. Stewart, *Greek Sculp-*

ture: An Exploration (New Haven, 1990), pp. 192–193; A. Ajootian in *Pity and Power in Ancient Athens* (Cambridge, 2005), pp. 246–248; V. M. Strocka in *Thiasos: Festschrift für Edwin Pochmarski zum 65. Geburtstag* (Vienna, 2008), pp. 1005–1015; G. I. Despinis, *AA* 2009, pp. 11–19.

TORSO OF A YOUTH

The torso of fine Pentelic marble and of about two-thirds life size (S 1313: late 5th–early 4th century B.C.) against the wall opposite Column 11 lacks a head, both arms, and both legs below the knees. The figure is well finished all around, and its surface shows little weathering. Despite its mutilated state the work impresses one by the beauty of its stance and modeling and by the sensitive finish of the marble. The weight was borne by the right leg, the missing left foot was thrust far back, and the head was turned slightly to the proper left. In the absence of attributes, identification would be hazardous; Herakles is just one of many possibilities. The statue is of interest, however, as an excellent example of the Athenian handling of a sculptural theme of which the most famous renderings were by Polykleitos. Stylistically the work could be as early as the 430s, and its technique indicates a date in the 5th or 4th century B.C. Found in a Christian tomb southwest of the Middle Stoa, its original provenience is unknown.

H. A. Thompson, *Hesperia* 18 (1949), pp. 233–234; H. von Heintze, *RM* 72 (1965) 19, 36–40; *Agora* XIV (1972), p. 148, n. 152.

TORSO OF A YOUTH

Just opposite that statue (S 1313), set next to Column 11, is a still more fragmentary torso of Classical date, made of Pentelic marble (S 502: 4th century B.C.). It was found by the excavators in two fragments in disturbed contexts near the middle of the Agora. There remains only the trunk of a figure of much the same scale and in much the same stance as the previous statue, but the head was slightly inclined to the proper right, and the right arm was raised high as though the hand had rested on the head.

GROUP OF TWO FEMALE FIGURES

Against the wall, on a high pedestal opposite Column 11, is a group in Parian marble comprising two adult female figures of about three-quarters life size (S 429: ca. 420 B.C.). The one carries the other high on her back. Both heads, all four legs, and three of the arms are missing. The sculpture has been terribly battered, and the back has been heavily worn by foot traffic.

The two figures have been skillfully differentiated in the choice of dress and in the treatment of the drapery: the lower figure wears a *peplos* of heavy material; the upper has a *chiton* of thin, clinging fabric. The group was carefully finished all around, the back as well as the front. The execution is of high quality. The style indicates a date of ca. 420 B.C.

The marble was found at a level of the Byzantine period in the filling of an ancient well to the east of the Hephaisteion ❶. In marble, scale, and quality the group would be appropriate to one of the pedimental compositions of the temple, probably, and in view of its place of finding, the east pediment. The meaning of the action in the sculpture is still enigmatic. Perhaps one is rescuing her friend in distress, or it is a depiction of *ephedrismos,* a game played with one person on the back of another.

H. A. Thompson, *Hesperia* 18 (1949), pp. 235–236; *Agora* XIV (1972), p. 148; A. De-livorrias, *Attische Giebelskulpturen und Akrotere des fünften Jahrhunderts* (Tübingen, 1974), pp. 33–40; C. Scheffer, *OpAth* 21 (1996), pp. 169–188.

FRAGMENT OF A MONUMENT FOR A VICTORY OF THE TRIBE LEONTIS IN A CAVALRY CONTEST (*ANTHIPPASIA*)

On a square pedestal opposite Column 12 is a fragment from the lower corner of a two-sided marble relief (Fig. 28; I 7167: early 4th century B.C.). The obverse preserves in whole or in part five horsemen. The riders are youthful, smoothfaced, bare headed, and clad in knee-length chitons. The commanding officer, who rides at the outer end of the line, is more mature: he is bearded and wears a helmet. Drilled holes in the appropriate places indicate that each of the men carried a single spear, made separately of bronze. The officer also carried a sword, the hilt of which appears above his left hand. The reins must have been rendered in paint, if at all.

On the reverse is the inscription: "The tribe Leontis won the victory." To the left there remains a leg and the tail of a lion, a punning allusion to the name of the tribe (λέων = lion). The event likely was a contest among the 10 tribes; the riders on the obverse are to be

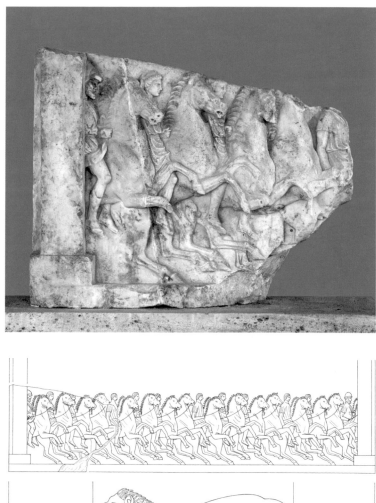

*Figure 28. Equestrian victory monument, early 4th century B.C., photograph
and restored drawing*

Figure 29. Monument base by Bryaxis, 4th century B.C., now in the National Archaeological Museum in Athens

regarded as a tribal contingent led by their tribal cavalry commander (*phylarchos*). The *anthippasia,* a mock cavalry battle held during the Greater Panathenaic Games, was the contest in which the victory was won.

The relief was carved close to the time when Xenophon was writing his two essays *The Cavalry Commander* and *On Horsemanship* (ca. 365 B.C.). One feels that Xenophon would have approved of both the style of the riders of Leontis and the rendering by the anonymous sculptor: "This is the attitude in which artists represent the horses on which gods and heroes ride, and men who manage such horses gracefully have a magnificent appearance" (*On Horsemanship* 11.8).

The relief is of Pentelic marble and was found reused in a late foundation to the west of the Royal Stoa ㉖, close to the site of the Bryaxis base (Fig. 29; see the *Agora Site Guide*, p. 108). That base, now in the National Museum, also came from a monument commemorative of victories won in equestrian contests. Although the present monument is a tribal dedication, the Bryaxis monument was of a more private nature, honoring as it did a man and his two sons, all of whom had led their teams to victory in the *anthippasia.*

T. L. Shear Jr., *Hesperia* 40 (1971), pp. 271–272; *Agora* XIV (1972), p. 95, n. 72; *AgPicBk* 24 (1998), pp. 28–30; *AgPicBk* 25 (2003), pp. 24–25; J. McK. Camp II in *The Athenian Agora: New Perspectives on an Ancient Site* (Mainz, 2009), pp. 30–31.

FRAGMENTS OF RELIEFS POSSIBLY FROM THE TEMPLE OF ARES

The four female figures (S 676, S 679, S 870, S 1072: 435–420 B.C.) exhibited against the wall opposite Column 13 are selected from a group of 40 or more fragments sufficiently uniform in scale and style to be attributed to a common source. All are of Pentelic marble, in high relief, and of the finest quality. The style indicates a date in the 430s B.C. Much of the frieze must have been occupied by quietly standing figures. Among the fragments not exhibited are several heads including one of a bearded male, a seated figure, and a piece with the heads of sheep—presumably sacrificial victims. The full height of the standing figures was about 0.85 m. In characterizing his figures the designer has introduced great variety: in the stance (*en face*, profile, three-quarter poses), in the choice of garments, and in the way they are worn.

The fragments have been found widely scattered throughout the excavation, but with many concentrated around the Temple of Ares ❸❽.

H. A. Thompson, *Hesperia* 21 (1952), pp. 94–95; B. Schlörb, *Untersuchungen zur Bild-hauergeneration nach Phidias* (Waldsassen, 1964), pp. 34–36; J. Travlos, *Pictorial Dictionary of Ancient Athens* (London, 1971), fig. 144; E. B. Harrison in *Archaische und klassische griechische Plastik* 2 (Mainz, 1986), pp. 109–117.

TORSO OF ATHENA

Opposite Column 14 stands the upper part of a torso of Athena carved in Pentelic marble (S 654: ca. 420 B.C.). The aegis is reduced to a diagonal strap supporting the head of Medusa. The snakes' heads that bordered the aegis were of bronze and have been wrenched from their sockets; on the back of the figure the writhing serpents are worked in the marble. The right arm of the goddess was extended, presumably to hold her spear; the left hung down, probably to rest on her shield. The style points to a date of ca. 420–410 B.C.; the scale and quality of the statue attest to its importance.

The torso was found in a Byzantine wall 18 m south of the Temple of Ares ❸❽. It may be the statue of Athena seen by Pausanias (1.8.4) in the sanctuary of Ares and attributed by him to "a man of Paros, Lokros by name." This sculptor is otherwise unknown.

T. L. Shear, *AJA* 40 (1936), pp. 196, 198; B. Schlörb, *Untersuchungen zur Bildhauergeneration nach Phidias* (Waldsassen, 1964), p. 35; G. Despinis, Συμβολή στη μελέτη του έργου του Αγορακρίτου (Athens, 1971), pp. 186–188; *Agora* XIV (1972), p. 164; *AgPicBk* 27 (2006), pp. 29–30.

STANDING FEMALE FIGURE

The life-size female torso of Pentelic marble (S 339: 4th century B.C.) opposite Columns 15 and 16 is clad in *chiton* and *peplos*. The long *kolpos* (the fold of the *peplos* over the chest) and overfold permit a rich treatment of the drapery on front and back. The left leg thrust well forward and the right knee slightly bent suggest a striding movement toward the spectator. Since the hair falls in a broad heavy mass down the very middle of the back, the head must have looked straight ahead. The head itself, now missing, was worked separately and set in a socket. Both forearms also were cut separately and attached by dowels, of which only the sockets remain; in both cases the arms were thrust forward. The upper part of the statue is heavily weathered from long exposure. The style points to a date in the first half of the 4th century B.C. The high quality of the carving and the heavy weathering indicate that the statue is an original work rather than a copy of Roman times.

The statue was found in the Great Drain ⑪ west of the Temple of Ares ㊳. Like the statue of Hadrian ⑯, this figure also had been reused in Late Antiquity as a cover slab on the drain.

T. L. Shear, *Hesperia* 4 (1935), pp. 372–374; L. J. Roccos, *Hesperia* 69 (2000), p. 258.

MONUMENT BASE FOR A PRIZE IN CHARIOT RACING (*APOBATES*)

The low base of Pentelic marble (Fig. 30; S 399: 4th century B.C.) opposite Columns 16 and 17 once carried a prize won in the *apobates* race at the Panathenaic Festival by the man whose name appears in the top band: Krates, son of Heortios, of Peiraeus. In the top of the block are a square socket for the post that held the prize and two smaller rectangular sockets for additional objects. The event itself is illustrated in the relief: the armed passenger was required to dismount and mount

Figure 30. Sculpted base for a monument celebrating a victory in the apobates
at the Panathenaic Games, 4th century B.C. *As the race followed the Panathenaic
Way, the armed passenger was expected to jump on and off the moving chariot.*

again while the chariot was in full motion. Harking back to the days of
Homeric warfare, this event was accounted by Athenian tradition the
earliest in the roster of the Panathenaic games; this in part accounts
for its prominence in the Parthenon frieze. The race was run on the
Panathenaic Way **37** in the Agora with the finish near the Eleusinion
56, and the victor's monument may be supposed to have been set up
near that racecourse. The style of the sculpture and of the lettering
points to a date in the early 4th century B.C.

The base was found in the Post-Herulian Wall **49** south of the
Stoa of Attalos and a little below the Eleusinion.

T. L. Shear, *Hesperia* 4 (1935), pp. 379–381; J. Travlos, *Pictorial Dictionary of Ancient
Athens* (London, 1971), fig. 26; *Agora* XIV (1972), p. 121; *AgPicBk* 24 (1998), p. 27;
AgPicBk 25 (2003), pp. 24–25; J. McK. Camp II in *The Athenian Agora: New Perspec-
tives on an Ancient Site* (Mainz, 2009), pp. 30–31.

STATUE OF A GODDESS FROM THE ROYAL STOA

Against the wall opposite Column 18 is a female torso of Pentelic marble about 1½ times life size (Fig. 31; S 2370: 350–325 B.C.). The head, now missing, was worked separately and set in a socket. The left forearm was likewise cut from a separate piece and secured with a dowel. This forearm is missing, as is the whole of the right arm and the legs below the knees. The figure rested its weight on the left leg; the left forearm was thrust forward. The goddess wears a sleeved *chiton* of thin and crinkly material. Her girdle, a thin cord, is looped over each shoulder, crossed behind and tied in front. Above the *chiton* is a voluminous *himation* thrown over the left shoulder and drawn diagonally across the front of the figure to be held between left forearm and waist. The outer garment is readily distinguished by its heavier, smoother fabric and by occasional fold marks. The statue is fully finished in the round. A date in the third quarter of the 4th century is made probable by the proportions of the figure, the massing of the drapery, the treatment of the crinkly *chiton*, and by the high quality of the carving.

Figure 31. Colossal statue of an allegorical figure, possibly Themis, found in front of the Royal Stoa, second half of the 4th century B.C.

For the restoration of the figure the best evidence is provided by the Themis from Rhamnous, a work of the third century B.C. by the local artist Chairestratos (Fig. 32). One likely explanation for the dependence of the Rhamnous statue on the Athenian one in its sculptural type is an identity of subject. The statue probably stood in front of the Royal Stoa ㉖ (Fig. 33), and for this position there could have been no more appropriate choice than the goddess who was the very personification of law and at the same time the protectress of oaths.

*Figure 32. Statue of Themis from Rhamnous, ca. 300 B.C.,
now in the National Archaeological Museum in Athens*

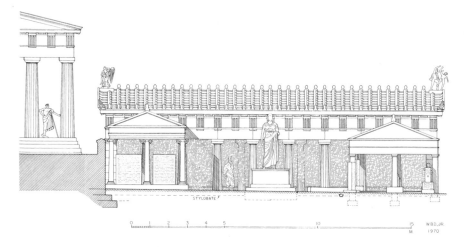

Figure 33. Restored elevation of the Royal Stoa, seen from the east, ca. 300 B.C., with the statue of "Themis" shown in front

However, Demokratia or Tyche (the sister of Themis) are also reasonable candidates for the statue's identification.

T. L. Shear, *Hesperia* 40 (1971), pp. 270–271; O. Palagia, *Hesperia* 51 (1982), pp. 99–113; O. Palagia in *The Archaeology of Athens and Attica under the Democracy* (Oxford, 1994), pp. 113–122.

PORTRAIT BUST OF ANTONINUS PIUS

Opposite Column 19 is a slightly greater-than-life-size marble bust (S 2436: A.D. 138–161) of the Emperor Antoninus Pius (A.D. 138–161). The Emperor wore armor (as shown by the epaulettes), below it a *chiton*, and over it a heavy fringed cloak. This portrait depicts the Emperor in his later years.

The bust was carved from a white marble with large and widely spaced crystals. It was found in a well in the Omega House 58.

T. L. Shear Jr., *Hesperia* 42 (1973), pp. 170–171.

STANDING MALE PORTRAIT STATUES

Opposite Column 20 are exhibited two examples of a type of male portrait statue common in Greece in the Roman period (S 850 + S 1604: 2nd century A.D. [body], ca. 300 A.D. [head]; S 936: 2nd century A.D.). Each figure wears a *chiton* or undergarment that is almost entirely concealed beneath a voluminous *himation* or mantle. Beside the left ankle of S 936 are the remains of a book box (*scrinium*). These and five other statues of the same period (three standing, two seated) were found to the east of the Odeion **41**; they were probably set up at the time of the reconstruction of the Odeion ca. A.D. 150, and may well have carried portrait heads of some of the men of letters associated with that building when it was used as a lecture hall. All are of Pentelic marble.

The head of a middle-aged man (S 1604) was inset by the excavators into the body of S 850 in 1957 (Fig. 34), but it is of later date (ca. 300 A.D.).

Figure 34. Portrait statue with inset head of later date

Agora I (1953) nos. 52, 57, 58; *Agora* XXIV (1988), p. 65.

PORTRAIT STATUE OF A MAGISTRATE

This stolid male figure (S 657: 5th century A.D.) stands at the end of the hall and wears undertunic, overtunic, and toga in the formal manner proper to a high civic official of late Imperial times (photo p. 11, upper right). The marble is Pentelic, the scale life-sized. Head, hands, and feet are missing, but the battering to which the statue has been subjected does not detract from what was its chief point of sculptural interest: the patterned and largely linear quality of the drapery which recalls the beginnings of Greek monumental sculpture in the

Early Archaic period (ca. 700–600 B.C.). This piece in fact completes the cycle of sculptural development in Greece; dating from the 5th century A.D., it is one of the latest statues in the round surviving from ancient Athens. It was found near the northeast corner of the Late Roman Palace ㊶.

Agora I (1953), no. 64, pp. 79–81; *AgPicBk* 5 (1960), fig. 19; A. Franz, *DOP* 19 (1965), p. 192; *Agora* XXIV (1988), pp. 65, 112–113.

🔹 At the end of the first floor there is an alcove beneath the staircase. The marble bench at the foot of the walls commands a pleasing view of the colonnade with its two very different series of columns and a prospect of the distant hills.

AKROTERION OF WINGED VICTORY (NIKE) FROM THE STOA OF ZEUS

Figure 35. Discovery of the winged Nike from the Stoa of Zeus in 1933 (above) and the Nike today (at right)

A statue of Victory (Nike) in Pentelic marble is set against the north wall of the Stoa (Fig. 35; S 312: ca. 400 B.C.). This statue was recovered in front of the Stoa of Zeus ㉕. Since the type and the heavy overall weathering are appropriate to an akroterion—a rooftop ornament—the statue might have stood on the roof of the building, probably at the left-hand angle of the south wing. Figural akroteria are unusual on stoas, but this stoa was dedicated to Zeus, and Nike, as messenger of the gods, was frequently associated with him.

The flamboyant sculptural style that was developed to such perfection at Athens in the generation after the Parthenon pediments was never more effectively employed than here. The

akroteria, as the latest elements in the Stoa of Zeus, date from the turn of the 5th and 4th centuries B.C. Many fragments of the wings of this figure and various parts of other Nikai were found in front of the Stoa. An alternative location on the Temple of Ares ❸❽ has also been suggested for this statue.

T. L. Shear, *Hesperia* 4 (1935), pp. 374–379; H. A. Thompson, *Hesperia* 6 (1937), p. 37; J. Travlos, *Pictorial Dictionary of Ancient Athens* (London, 1971), fig. 671; *Agora* XIV (1972), p. 99; A. Delivorrias, *Attische Giebelskulpturen und Akrotere des fünften Jahrunderts* (Tübingen, 1974), pp. 124–125, 137–142, 160–161; E. B. Harrison in *Πρακτικά του XII Διεθνούς Συνεδρίου Κλασικής Αρχαιολογίας Γ΄* (Athens, 1988), p. 104; *AgPicBk* 27 (2006), front cover, fig. 32, fig. 49; C. A. Mauzy in *The Athenian Agora: New Perspectives on an Ancient Site* (Mainz, 2009), p. 95.

ORIGINAL FLOORING OF THE STOA OF ATTALOS AND MOSAIC FLOOR

A sample of ancient flooring that was found in this part of the building has been preserved beside the northernmost interior column. It was made of marble chips imbedded in mortar. A similar type of flooring has been used in the restoration.

Next to this flooring lie two sections of mosaic floor (Fig. 36; A 2103 and A 2105) from a room in a large house of the 4th century A.D. outside the southwest corner of the Agora along the west slope of the Areopagus ❼❹. The figured scene that must have occupied the square panel has been almost entirely destroyed; there remain only the elaborate geometric borders worked out in strong colors with tesserae of marble, limestone, and glass.

H. A. Thompson, *Hesperia* 17 (1948), pp. 169–170; B. Tsakirgis in *The Art of Antiquity* (Athens, 2007), pp. 270–271.

🔄 Continue along the colonnade heading southward, passing the objects viewed in concert with their associated pieces next to the wall.

INSCRIBED VOTIVE *STELE* WITH A SCENE OF A COBBLER'S WORKSHOP

The tall pillar of blue marble (Fig. 37; I 7396: 4th century B.C.) set against Column 20 has a slot in its top that once supported the offering proper, probably a marble relief with a cult scene. This monument

Figure 36. Mosaic floor from the house outside the southwest corner of the Agora, 4th century A.D., with watercolor showing its polychromy

Figure 37. Cobbler's workshop, votive stele dedicated by the shoemaker Dionysios to the hero Kallistephanos, first half of the 4th century B.C.

is unusual in that even the top panel of the pedestal is decorated with a scene in low relief. Here is a glimpse into the shoemaking shop of Dionysios, the dedicator. There are in all five figures of whom at least one is bearded and elderly, one is a young man, and one a child. All sit on high-backed chairs except for the child, who must be content with a stool. All are evidently engaged in the making of shoes, and a varied display of their products hangs from pegs set into a bracket on the wall above their heads.

The text, which begins on the band beneath the relief and continues on the shaft below, records first the dedication of the offering by Dionysios and his children to the hero Kallistephanos (Well-crowned) and his children, in terms that recall scenes of worship on many reliefs dedicated by families to Asklepios and his children. Then in hexameter verse Dionysios relates that in response to a vision in his sleep he is now honoring the hero and the hero's children. In return he asks the hero for wealth and good health. A date in the second quarter of the 4th century B.C. suits the style of the relief and the letter forms. The hero Kallistephanos is otherwise unknown. The relief is a relatively new addition to the few known illustrations of the Classical period showing tradesmen at work. The shaft was found to the southeast of the Stoa of Attalos.

J. McK. Camp II, *AJA* 77 (1973), p. 209; J. McK. Camp II, *The Athenian Agora* (London, 1986), pp. 146–147; J. McK. Camp II in *Greek Art in View* (Oxford, 2004), pp. 129–137.

BASE OF A STATUE OF THE PHILOSOPHER KARNEADES

The low base of Hymettian marble (*IG* II² 3781: 2nd century B.C.) against Column 19 once supported a seated statue of bronze; note the two holes in its top for dowels to secure the feet. The inscription on the front reads:

> *Attalos and Ariarathes of the township of Sypalettos*
> *dedicated (this statue of) Karneades of the township of Azenia.*

The man honored was the head of the New Academy, the leading philosopher in Athens of the 2nd century B.C. While serving as head of a delegation sent by the Athenians to plead a case before the Roman senate in 156–155 B.C., Karneades had given a series of lectures on Greek philosophy which made a lasting impression on the intellectual life of Rome. This is likely the statue of Karneades that was seen and commended as a good likeness by Cicero (*de Finibus* 5.2.4), and that served as a prototype for many later copies.

There is some debate about the identity of the dedicators. Although Attalos and Ariarathes were once identified as royals from Pergamon and Cappadocia, respectively, it is now more widely believed that they were Athenian-born citizens who bore the same names.

H. A. Thompson, *Hesperia* 19 (1950), pp. 318–319; *AgPicBk* 2 (1959; reprinted 1992), figs. 34, 35; B. D. Meritt, *The Athenian Year* (Berkeley, 1961), pp. 229–230; G. M. Richter, *Portraits of the Greeks* 2 (London, 1965), p. 250; H. B. Mattingly, *Historia* 20 (1971), pp. 29–32; *Agora* XIV (1972), p. 107; C. Habicht, *Hesperia* 59 (1990), pp. 571–572; S. V. Tracy and C. Habicht, *Hesperia* 60 (1991), p. 217; A. Stähli, *AA* 1991, pp. 219–252.

PORTRAIT HEAD, POSSIBLY HERODOTOS

The bald and bearded head (S 270: 2nd century A.D.) set against Column 18 is a portrait of a distinguished intellectual of the Classical period. The features correspond closely with inscribed portraits of Herodotos, although the baldness would be unusual; it is doubtful that it is a likeness of the "Father of History." Copied in the 2nd century A.D. from an early original, it perhaps adorned a library.

T. L. Shear, *Hesperia* 4 (1935), pp. 402–404; *Agora* I (1953), no. 1, pp. 9–10; *AgPicBk* 5 (1960), fig. 2; G. M. Richter, *The Portraits of the Greeks* 1 (London, 1965), pp. 146–147.

RECORD OF A SETTLEMENT BY A BOARD OF ARBITRATORS CONCERNING SALAMINIAN SACRIFICES

This long and complete inscription on Pentelic marble (I 3244: 363/2 B.C.) set against Column 17 records the decisions handed down by a board of five private arbitrators in the year 363/2 B.C. The matter at issue was the administration of sacrifices made to various divinities and heroes by two branches of the clan of Salaminioi. The document is very illuminating not only for the mechanics of ancient religious practice but also for the process of arbitration, an important part of Athenian justice. The *stele* was to be set up in Athens in the Sanctuary of Eurysakes, one of the principal heroes of Salamis; the Eurysakeion was located to the south of the Hephaisteion (see the *Agora Site Guide*, p. 42).

W. S. Ferguson, *Hesperia* 7 (1938), pp. 1–74; *Agora* III (1957; reprinted 1973), no. 254; Sokolowski, *Lois sacreés des cités grecques: Supplément* (Paris, 1962), no. 19; *Agora* XIX (1991), no. L4a; R. Parker, *Athenian Religion* (Oxford, 1996), pp. 308–316; M. C. Taylor, *Salamis and the Salaminioi* (Amsterdam, 1997), pp. 47–63; S. D. Lambert, *ZPE* 119 (1997), pp. 85–106.

ANNUAL REPORT OF THE STATE AUCTIONEERS (*POLETAI*)

A perfectly preserved inscription (I 5509: 367/6 B.C.) standing against Column 16 contains the report of the board of eight public auctioneers (*poletai*) for the year 367/6 B.C. Their activities comprised the sale of a confiscated house and the leasing of 17 mining properties in the Laureion area.

Hesperia Suppl. 4 (1940), p. 59; M. Crosby, *Hesperia* 10 (1941), pp. 14–27; M. Crosby, *Hesperia* 19 (1950), pp. 189–206; *Hesperia* Suppl. 9 (1951), pp. 150–154; *AgPicBk* 4 (1960), fig. 6; J. McK. Camp II, *The Athenian Agora* (London, 1986), pp. 130–131, *Agora* XIX (1991), no. P5; *Hesperia* Suppl. 29 (1998), p. 64; S. D. Lambert, *The Phratries of Attica* (Ann Arbor, revised 1998), no. T10; P. J. Rhodes and R. Osborne, *Greek Historical Inscriptions* (Oxford, 2003), no. 36.

PRYTANY DECREE

The marble inscription (I 1024: 260/59 B.C.) set against Column 15 has never been separated from its ancient base. It illustrates the normal way in which these tall *stelai* were secured with molten lead in a slot cut in the top of a heavy block of rough stone which was let down into the earth almost to its full depth. The text records votes of thanks to the *prytaneis,* i.e., to the members of the Council of Five Hundred who had served as presiding officers in the past year, and to various officials of the Council. The inscription was found just to the east of the Tholos ❺, the headquarters of the *prytaneis.* It dates probably from 260/59 B.C.

Hesperia Suppl. 1 (1937), no. 9; *Agora* XV (1974), no. 86; S. V. Tracy, *Hesperia* 57 (1988), pp. 305, 307; A. S. Henry, *Chiron* 18 (1988), pp. 217–222.

STATUE OF VENUS GENETRIX TYPE, POSSIBLY A NYMPH

The small, headless torso (S 1654: 2nd century A.D.) that stands against Column 13 is an adaptation made in the Roman period of a famous Athenian original of the late 5th century B.C., the so-called Venus Genetrix. The surface has suffered from proximity to a cesspool. The goddess wears a thin *chiton* that has slipped down over her left shoulder and breast; her back is covered by a *himation* that was held up by her (now missing) right hand. In the left hand is a water pitcher, replacing an apple in the original. The statue was found in front of the Nymphaion ⓬ for which it was probably made; the date should therefore be the middle of the 2nd century A.D.

H. A. Thompson, *Hesperia* 22 (1953), pp. 53–54; *AgPicBk* 11 (1968), fig. 3.

HEAD OF VICTORY (NIKE)

The well-preserved head of Pentelic marble (S 2354: 2nd century A.D.), slightly over life-size, set against Column 12, is a copy, carved probably in the 2nd century A.D., of a work of the second half of the 5th century B.C. The prototype was very similar to—but not quite identical with—the Nike of Paionios at Olympia. It was found in the Omega House ㊽.

T. L. Shear Jr., *Hesperia* 40 (1971), p. 273; E. B. Harrison in *The Eye of Greece* (Cambridge, 1982), pp. 53–65.

🔄 Bypass the male torso S 502, already viewed in conjunction with its companion S 1313 against the Stoa wall (p. 45).

TRIPOD BASE

Between Columns 6 and 7 stands the Pentelic marble base (photo p. 11, top left; S 370: 2nd century B.C.) for a bronze tripod. The bowl of the tripod rested on top of the marble; its bronze legs were set against the thin edges of the marble in such a way as to frame the sculptured panels. The tripod was presumably a prize won in a competition for drama or the dithyramb (a choral song and dance also in honor of Dionysos). The nude male figure with a knotted club has been identified as Theseus, prince of Athens. He appears to have been the central figure, and so is perhaps the hero of the piece. To the right he is flanked by a regal draped male (perhaps King Aigeus, father of Theseus), to the left by a draped female figure with a flat bowl used to pour liquid offerings called a *phiale* (possibly Medea, wife of Aigeus). Dating probably from the 2nd century B.C., the base is an early and important example of the Neo-Attic style. The highly mannered revival of such archaic features as patterned drapery, a mincing stride, and imperfect anatomy appear in startling contrast with contemporary realism in the rendering of Theseus's cloak.

The base was found standing upright in the middle of the principal room of the Civic Offices ㉑, surrounded by the debris from the destruction of the building in A.D. 267. Since there was no proper underpinning, this could not have been its original position.

T. L. Shear, *Hesperia* 4 (1935), pp. 324, 387–393; W. Fuchs, *Die Vorbilder der neuattischen Reliefs* (Berlin, 1959), pp. 46, 166, 171; *Agora* XI (1965), pp. 79–81, no. 128; J. Travlos, *Pictorial Dictionary of Ancient Athens* (London, 1971), p. 234; *Agora* XIV (1972), pp. 79, 126.

TORSO OF A RECLINING MALE FIGURE

Against Column 6 is the upper part of a male figure nearly two-thirds life size, of Pentelic marble, reclining with the support of its left arm (Fig. 38; S 147: 2nd century B.C.). The attitude recalls the figure of the Ilissos River from the west pediment of the Parthenon, and the torso was at one time assigned tentatively to the corresponding position in the east pediment of the Hephaisteion. However, the emphatic modeling and the use of Pentelic rather than Parian marble appear to exclude it from the Hephaisteion. The torso may derive from a

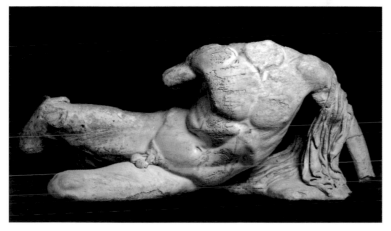

Figure 38. Reclining male figure, 2nd century B.C. (top); Ilissos River figure from the west pediment of the Parthenon, now in the British Museum (bottom).

reclining Herakles of Hellenistic date. It was recovered from a modern foundation to the east of the Hephaisteion.

H. A. Thompson, *Hesperia* 18 (1949), p. 233; *Agora* XIV (1972), p. 148, n. 152.

BOUNDARY STONES (*HOROI*)

The tour of the objects in the colonnade concludes with two boundary stones (Fig. 39; I 5510, I 7039: ca. 500 B.C.) next to columns 3 (I 5510 = *IG* I³ 1087) and 4 (I 7039 = *IG* I³ 1088). Both monuments were found in situ at the southwest corner of the Agora ❿, I 5510 next to the house of Simon the Cobbler ❾, I 7039 beneath the west end of the Middle Stoa ㊆. These markers and others like them served to indicate the separation between private space and the public space of the Agora square and to warn those who were forbidden entrance, such as certain types of criminals and people not yet of age.

Both rectangular shafts are of Parian marble and inscribed along the top and a side with the same message: "I am the boundary of the Agora." The letter forms date the inscriptions to ca. 500 B.C., a time before the Greek alphabet or its direction of writing were fully standardized. One may note that the writing of I 7039 runs from right to left, the opposite of I 5510.

I 5510: T. L. Shear, *Hesperia* 8 (1938), pp. 205–206; *Hesperia* Suppl. 4 (1940), pp. 107–108; *Agora* III (1957, reprinted 1973), no. 713. Both *horoi*: H. A. Thompson, *Hesperia* 37 (1968), pp. 61–63; J. Travlos, *Pictorial Dictionary of Ancient Athens* (London, 1971), figs. 20–22; *Agora* XIV (1972), pp. 117–119; J. McK. Camp II, *The Athenian Agora* (London, 1986), pp. 48, 51–52; *Agora* XIX (1991), nos. H25, H26; *Hesperia* Suppl. 31 (2003), pp. 289–291; *AgPicBk* 4 (revised 2004), p. 5; G. V. Lalonde, *Hesperia* 75 (2006), pp. 86–88.

GROUND FLOOR: AREA OF SHOPS

🎟 Of the 21 shops on the ground floor of the Stoa, three at the south end (B–D) and one at the north end (U) have been restored to their original form. Ten shops have been merged to form a continuous museum gallery. Begin at the south end.

MEMORIAL ROOM

(normally closed to the public)

Three bronze plaques on the back wall commemorate the excavation of the Agora, the rebuilding of the Stoa of Attalos, and the landscaping of the area. The record includes the names of those who participated in the work and of those who contributed money. A bronze medallion on the right wall honors John D. Rockefeller Jr. (1874–1960) as the first

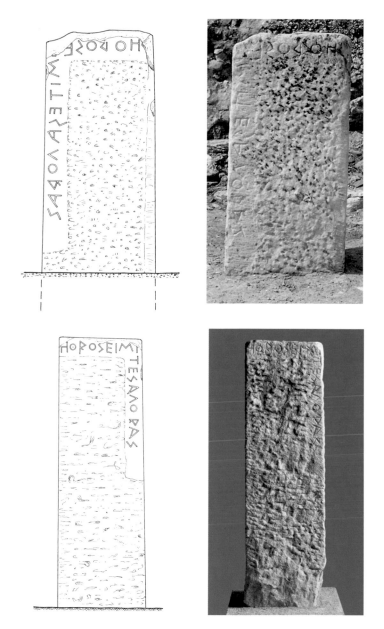

Figure 39. Agora boundary stones, ca. 500 B.C.: (top) the stone under the west end of the Middle Stoa (I 7039, drawing and photo); (bottom) the stone southeast of the Tholos (I 5510, drawing and photo).

and principal donor. The mosaic floor is entirely modern; it is the kind of flooring that might have been found in such a room in antiquity.

Several pieces of marble sculpture are now stored here, including female figure S 182, which might have been an akroterion from the Hephaisteion (see the *Agora Site Guide*, pp. 40–41).

SALES ROOM

Guide books, picture books, postcards, and replicas of various objects are on sale. For other photographs and for the scientific publications relating to the Agora, enquire at the museum offices on the upper floor of the Stoa.

EXHIBITION OF ANCIENT WINE JARS

(if closed, ask the guards if entrance is possible)
The cuttings in the threshold and jambs of the doorway in Shop D are particularly illuminating for understanding how the ancient doors operated. Note the cuttings for the single bar used for fastening the original doors that were set in line with the inner face of the wall. Later, after the insertion of a mezzanine floor, the doors were moved to the outer edge of the threshold. In this period there were cuttings

for six bars on the inside and for one on the outside. The wear on the threshold shows that one normally entered on the right. Carved at eye level on the face of the right-hand jamb as one enters is the figure of Hermes, god of commerce: a clear indication of the use of this room (Fig. 40).

For the transport of wine the Greeks used a terracotta jar (*amphora*) that commonly held as much as a man could conveniently carry, i.e., 19–30 liters (5–8 gallons). The bottom of the jar was pointed and shaped to fit the hand; a stout handle on either side facilitated lifting and pouring. The jar was stoppered by means of

Figure 40. Herm carved on the doorway of Shop D

a terracotta disk secured with plaster, or occasionally by a cork. While the clay was still soft, a seal was commonly impressed on the top of the handle. The occurrence of the names of magistrates as well as of manufacturers in these seals is a reminder that in those Greek states in which wine was a significant article of commerce, the trade was rigorously controlled by the government. Frequently the stamps also indicate the place of origin, either explicitly by word (e.g., Knidian, Thasian) or by a familiar symbol such as the rose of Rhodes.

The Agora excavations have yielded just over 800 amphoras that were more or less complete (Fig. 41) and over 15,000 stamped handles (Fig. 42). Because in most cases the country of origin is now known, and because the dates can normally be fixed to within a half-century, the wine trade has become the best-documented chapter in the history of ancient commerce. The jars found in the Agora come from many parts of the Aegean, especially from Thasos, Chios, Rhodes, Kos, and Knidos, but also from as far afield as the Black Sea, Italy, and Spain. The range in time is from the 6th century B.C. to the 6th century A.D. On the shelves of the left side of the room the jars are arranged in chronological sequence, beginning below with the plump and well-rounded shapes of the Archaic period, progressing through the crisply profiled forms of Hellenistic times, and ending at the upper right with some "dagger-shaped" amphoras of late antiquity.

On the right side of the room the arrangement is by place of origin. Here are represented all the famous wines of Greek antiquity. The most distinguished, and most costly, were those from Chios and Thasos. Cheaper and much more common were the Rhodian and Knidian wines. Each of the important wine-producing centers adopted early a characteristic shape of jar and clung to that shape for centuries as jealously as the modern makers of famous liqueurs and spirits. Note for instance the bulging neck of the Chian *amphora*, the ringed toe of the Knidian, and the double handle of the Koan.

In the table case are exhibited characteristic specimens of the stamped handles. In several instances the symbol that appears on the jar can be matched on the coins of the producing state: the rose of Rhodes, the sphinx of Chios, and Herakles, the favorite hero of Thasos. The importance of the wine trade to some of these states is further attested by the appearance of wine jars of characteristic local shape on their coins. An especially rich series of stamps comes from the north Aegean island of Thasos.

Figure 41. Wine amphoras (jars) in storage in the basement of the Stoa of Attalos

Figure 42. A Rhodian amphora stamp with the head of Helios and the name of the magistrate Sostratos

Photographs on the back wall illustrate the use and handling of wine jars in antiquity. Here, too, is a map with an indication of the principal centers of wine production and of wine consumption. The exhibition has been mounted with the aid of a contribution from the Achaia Clauss Wine Company in Patras, Greece.

Graffito Herm: *AgPicBk* 14 (1974; reprinted 1988), figs. 46, 47; B. Tsakirgis in *The Athenian Agora: New Perspectives on an Ancient Site* (Mainz, 2009), p. 54. **Amphoras**: V. Grace and M. Savvatianou-Petropoulakou in *Exploration Archéologique de Délos* XXVII (Paris, 1970), pp. 277–382; *AgPicBk* 6 (revised 1979); M. L. Lawall in *The Athenian Agora: New Perspectives on an Ancient Site* (Mainz, 2009), pp. 63–68.

🔰 From the south end of the Stoa, take the stairs to explore the display on the upper floor. Access by elevator for visitors with disabilities can be arranged with the museum guards.

SOUTH STAIRWELL

The first shop at the south end of the Stoa is now largely occupied by a restoration of the stairway of the Roman period designed to provide access to the upper floor. The walls of the room are for the most part ancient; set into their faces are many small sockets presumably for the support of shelving. Before taking the stairs, observe on the south wall of the Stoa, to the right of the doorway of Shop A, a man's head rudely incised (Fig. 43).

About halfway up the staircase is a landing. Here, a doorway was opened in the back wall of the Stoa when the stairway was built ca. A.D. 100 in order to allow visitors to leave the building and proceed to the Roman Agora to the southeast along a street lined with colonnades **47**. Through the modern grille one

Figure 43. Graffiti of the Stoa: man's head to the right of Shop A.

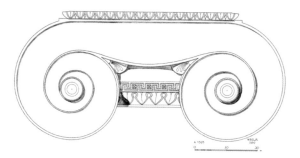

Figure 45. Ionic capital from the Temple of Athena at Sounion, mid-5th century B.C., photograph and restored drawing

with fragments of several others of the same series and a number of associated column drums, was found in the Post-Herulian Wall in the area of the Library of Pantainos ㊽. The fine-grained marble streaked with gray comes from Agrileza, near Sounion, and the capitals found in Athens are identical with one found among the ruins of the Temple of Athena at Sounion (now in the National Museum in Athens). The columns, together with parts of the entablature, were salvaged and brought to the Agora in the Early Roman period and reused in the Southeast Temple ㊼. Compare the history of the Temple of Ares ㊳ and the Southwest Temple ⑳.

A 2887: L. S. Meritt, *Hesperia* 65 (1996), pp. 140, 167–169, no. 21. **Column from Sounion**: W. B. Dinsmoor, *Hesperia* 51 (1982), pp. 429–438; L. S. Meritt, *Hesperia* 65 (1996), pp. 134, 158–163, no. 17A.

MODELS WITH VIEWS OF THE ANCIENT CITY

The height and position of the Stoa allow for excellent views of the topography and monuments of the city through the openings in the colonnade. The models of the Tholos, Acropolis, Pnyx, and the Agora in different periods on display here can be viewed in concert with the ancient remains.

Across from the Ionic column from Sounion is a model of the Tholos ❺. The roofing system is uncertain because of the round plan of the building and the diamond-shaped roof tiles that were used. This model shows a hypothetical reconstruction with an opening at the center; compare the closed roof of the model illustrated in the *Agora Site Guide,* Fig. 21. The Tholos is only just visible directly to the west through the trees. The model of the Acropolis set near the south end of the colonnade shows it as it was in the 2nd century A.D. The openings in the south end of the Stoa command a good view of the hill. The caves of Apollo and Pan can be distinguished in the cliffs below the Propylaia. Among the trees one may also catch glimpses of the Pana-thenaic Way and of the Post-Herulian Wall as they descend the steep slope side-by-side. The fortification wall is particularly well preserved in the final stretch immediately below the viewer to the south of the Stoa, where it overlies the west porch of the Library of Pantainos ㊽. Here, as usual, the wall was made entirely of material stripped from the ancient buildings destroyed in the Herulian sack of A.D. 267.

The next case holds models of the Pnyx illustrating two of the three periods of development of the political assembly place on the neighboring hill slope visible 500 m to the southwest.

The model on the bottom shelf of the case represents Period I (ca. 500 B.C.), in which the floor of the auditorium followed the natural slope of the hill. At the end of the 5th century B.C., the slope was reversed by means of an artificial embankment, intended perhaps to provide shelter against the winds.

Period II is not on display.

Period III (Fig. 46: second half of the 4th century B.C.) represents a monumental rebuilding on the same lines. Work was also begun at this time on two large colonnades on the hilltop for the convenience of those attending the assemblies. The building program was broken off by a threat of invasion toward the end of the 4th century, and a fortification wall was erected on the foundations of the colonnades.

Figure 46. Model of the Pnyx, Period III, second half of the 4th century B.C.

About 200 B.C., this wall was shifted to a stronger line on the brow of the hill as shown in the large model on the top shelf of the case.

Next are two models of the Agora, the first as it was ca. 500 B.C., then ca. 400 B.C. A third model representing the Agora as it was about the middle of the 2nd century A.D. will be viewed later near the center of the colonnade. By looking over the parapet of the Stoa, the visitor can identify the existing foundations of the various ancient buildings represented in the models.

Models of the Acropolis and Pynx: J. Travlos, *Pictorial Dictionary of Ancient Athens* (London, 1971), fig. 89 and pp. 466–475; *Agora* XIV (1972), pp. 48–50; *Hesperia* Suppl. XIX (1981), pp. 133–147; *AgPicBk* 4 (revised 2004), fig. 15. **Tholos model**: S. Miller in *Πρακτικά του ΧΙΙ Διεθνούς Συνεδρίου Κλασικής Αρχαιολογίας Δ΄* (Athens 1988), pp. 134–139.

STOA PARAPET

Just south of the two early Agora models, various original, ancient fragments are incorporated into the third column from the south end and the parapet crown of the adjacent bays. Cuttings in the parapet crown indicate that the openings between the columns could be closed by means of awnings against sun or wind. The ancient parapet was carved on both faces; in the restoration the inner face has been left plain except for the painted panels at both the south and north ends of the colonnade.

🔄 An exhibit of sculptures is presented along the remainder of the colonnade, set between the inner and outer columns so that most pieces can be viewed from multiple vantage points. They are arranged in groups that should be approached in a clockwise direction. Almost all are carved from the white marble referred to as "Pentelic" after the local marble quarry.

WORKS OF THE LATE CLASSICAL AND HELLENISTIC PERIOD (4TH CENTURY B.C. AND LATER): IDEALIZING IMAGES OF GODS AND MORTALS

The first part of the exhibit brings together sculptures from a variety of time periods, all of which have in common a classicizing style. New themes and subjects were introduced in the Late Classical and Hellenistic periods, but the idealism established in the 5th century B.C. continued to be replicated. Because later sculptures so often feature Classical traits, a thorough understanding of stylistic and technological changes is necessary to determine a proper date for pieces. New research often challenges old ideas.

STATUE OF A YOUNG WOMAN, PERHAPS ARTEMIS

The first sculpture encountered (S 440: possibly 4th–3rd century B.C.) is a female figure in Pentelic marble about two-thirds life size striding forward, clad in *chiton, peplos,* and *himation.* She lacks head, arms, and the front part of her left foot, which was cut separately. The characteristic movement, combined with heavy overall weathering, mark her as an akroterion. The statue was found just south of the Metroon ⓮. Although it has been dated to the Hellenistic period, it may instead be an Augustan work.

TORSO OF ARTEMIS BOULAIA

Although this female figure (S 912: 3rd–2nd century B.C.) is missing her head, forearms, and legs from the knees down, she can be identified as Artemis by the animal skin tied around her sleeved *chiton* at the waist. This statue was found near the Tholos ❺, so it is likely that she is Artemis Boulaia, who watched over the Council (*boule*). The chairmen (*prytaneis*) offered sacrifices to her before meetings.

Hesperia Suppl. 4 (1940), pp. 139–141.

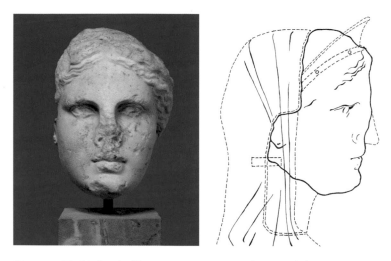

Figure 47. Marble head of Demeter, ca. 150 B.C., with restored drawing

HEAD OF AN OVER-LIFE-SIZE STATUE OF DEMETER

The slightly over-life-size female head of Parian marble set in front of Column 6 of the interior colonnade is now considered to be from a work of ca. 150 B.C. with classicizing features (Fig. 47; S 551). Behind the mass of wavy hair above the brow are a cutting and drilled holes for fastening a metal diadem. Deep cuttings farther back show that a garment was drawn up over the rear of the head like a veil. The ears are pierced for earrings. The ideal quality of the head, as well as the diadem and the veil, are appropriate to a goddess, in this case, Demeter. It is likely that its original location was the Eleusinion sanctuary **56**, just up the hill from the sculpture's findspot, where it was probably paired with a figure of Demeter's daughter, Kore (S 1874, not on display). It may be from the same workshop as Aphrodite Hegemone on display in the ground-floor colonnade (S 378, p. 38).

A. Stewart in *Regional Schools in Hellenistic Sculpture* (Oxford, 1998), pp. 83–92; A. Stewart, *Hesperia* 81 (2012), pp. 655–689.

FEMALE HEADS

The hair of the woman on the right (S 1308: 4th century B.C.) is tightly bound in a kerchief (*sakkos*). This head may have been broken off a

grave *stele* carved in high relief. The idealized female head on the left
(S 955: late 5th or early 4th century B.C.) with a mass of fluffy hair
gathered into a bun at the back and with ears drilled for earrings likely
represents a goddess. Similar in style to the sculptures of the Temple
of Ares (some of which are displayed on the ground floor, pp. 38,
41), it may date as early as 420 B.C.

S 955: T. L. Shear, *Hesperia* 7 (1938), pp. 350–351; A. Delivorrias, *Attische Giebelskulp-turen und Akrotere des fünften Jahrunderts* (Tübingen, 1974), pp. 109–110, 152–154.

FEMALE HEAD, POSSIBLY APHRODITE

This head of a woman (S 476: ca. 150–86 B.C.) features a groove carved
through the curls of the hair that once held a small metal crown, now
lost. The face is polished, but the right ear is uncarved. The head was
reused as packing material for a Roman wall, and the broken nose may
be a result of damage sustained during the Sullan siege of Athens in
86 B.C. It was discovered with other sculptures that copy Aphrodite
types, and this, too, may be an image of that goddess. It is now considered to be a Hellenistic piece with classicizing features.

H. A. Thompson, *Hesperia* 6 (1937), p. 168, n. 1; A. Stewart, *Hesperia* 81 (2012), pp.
298–306, 322–323.

HEADS OF YOUTHS

These two heads of life-size have in common the mild idealism of Late
Classical art. The upper right portion of the male head in the center
(S 591: 4th–3rd century B.C.) has been broken away. It is carved from
fine Parian marble and so undoubtedly belonged to a freestanding
statue, perhaps of a youthful divinity. It was uncovered in the same
Roman wall packing as the female head (S 476) to its right. The youthful male head on the left (S 212: 4th–3rd century B.C.) has the gentle
melancholy familiar from Attic grave monuments of the 4th century
B.C. The head was been reworked, however, in the Roman period:
note the joint for a patch on the right side, the drilling of the eyes, the
trimming of the lips, and the scarification of the hair above the left eye.

S 591: H. A. Thompson, *Hesperia* 6 (1937), p. 168, n. 1. **S 212**: T. L. Shear, *Hesperia* 2
(1933), pp. 528–531.

ROMAN COPIES OF CLASSICAL SCULPTURES (1ST–2ND CENTURY A.D.): THE ATHENIAN WORKSHOPS REPRODUCE CLASSICAL WORKS OF ART

Many of the Roman-period sculptures on display in the museum colonnades and gallery are copies of older Greek prototypes (see pp. 30–32 on marble copies and workshops). Because sculptors in Athens had a wide range of models at their disposal—Archaic, Classical, Late Classical, and Hellenistic—the pieces they produced, too, showed a remarkable variety of temporal and stylistic qualities. Unfinished sculptures and multiple copies harkening back to the same original provide insights into the creative process.

STATUE OF EROS

Although this standing boy lacks wings (S 902: 2nd century A.D.), the right arm draped across the body, the closed eyes, and the curly hair identify him as a sleeping Eros, the personification of love and son of Aphrodite. By the Hellenistic period it was usual to represent him as a child, and this piece is one of many later variants based on a work of the 4th century B.C. Just below the left hip a strut has been broken off, indicating either that the statue was originally part of a group or that the boy was leaning on a support.

T. L. Shear, *Hesperia* 7 (1938), pp. 351–352.

HEAD OF A GODDESS, PROBABLY PERSEPHONE

A Pentelic marble head of a goddess of slightly over life size is exhibited facing west (S 547: 2nd century A.D.). Her abundant hair is parted in the middle and drawn down to the right and left to overhang the forehead in heavy, wavy masses. On the back of the head the hair is gathered into a compact bunch that protrudes far out at the level of the ears and is encircled by a broad ribbon. The stump of a massive support rises from the top of the head. This is a copy made in the 2nd century A.D. of an original work of the Early Classical period whose fame is attested by the existence of several replicas. The identification is still problematic. The presence of the stump on top of this head and on one or two of the other replicas suggests that in the Roman period the figure was adapted to some architectural use as a caryatid or was made to carry a basket or the like.

HEADS OF MELEAGER

The next pair of heads are examples of copies taken from the same famous original, in this instance a statue of the type that was commonly used to represent the mythological hero Meleager, the great hunter. The type shows stylistic features that have been attributed to Skopas, a famous sculptor of the 4th century B.C.: characteristic is the massive squareness of the heads, the deep-set eyes, and the tousled hair with a small topknot at the middle of the front. The two copies differ from one another a good deal in the treatment of the side and back hair, although the pattern of locks framing the face is the same. S 2035 (right) may be of the second half of the 1st century A.D.; S 1227 (left) is probably of Augustan date. Both are of Pentelic marble.

E. B. Harrison, *Hesperia* 29 (1960), pp. 381–382.

HEAD OF ALEXANDER THE GREAT

The bust of sparkling, coarse-grained, bluish white Thasian marble (Fig. 48; S 2089: 2nd century A.D.), slightly over life-size, displayed facing north, comes from the Post-Herulian Wall in the area of the Southeast Stoa **51**; it probably originated in the sculpture workshops nearby. Of a curiously truncated shape, the bust proper rests on a rectangular plinth; the junction between the bust and plinth is masked by a row of acanthus leaves. Although complete, the work is unfinished: the surface retains the marks of the chisel and has not yet been rasped. Measuring points on the chin and on the hair above the eyes show that the sculptor was copying from another head. At least 10 other replicas of the type are known, most of them, like the present piece, dating from the 2nd century A.D.; another example, adapted to represent Helios the sun god, is displayed at the north end of the colonnade (Fig. 49; S 2355, p. 96).

The face is that of a young man: fresh, vigorous, yet romantic with a dramatic quality imparted by a slight twist of the neck, upturned gaze, deep-set eyes, and leonine hair, which is confined by a narrow headband. The bust retains the upper edge of a tunic. Through an

Figure 48 (left). Bust of Alexander the Great, 2nd century A.D.
Figure 49 (right). Bust of Helios, 2nd century A.D.

ill-founded early identification busts of this type have long been referred to as "Eubouleus," the Good Counselor, a god associated with the Eleusinian Mysteries. Instead, however, they exhibit the essential features of the young Alexander the Great as known from complete statues and from literary references. They may therefore be idealized portrayals of the youthful Alexander, interest in whose personality and iconography persisted throughout antiquity and rose to one of its periodic heights in Greece in the 2nd century A.D.

E. B. Harrison, *Hesperia* 29 (1960), pp. 382–389; S. Adam, *The Technique of Greek Sculpture in the Archaic and Classical Periods* (Oxford, 1966), pp. 36, 67; *AgPicBk* 27 (2006), p. 34.

🏃 Pause before the next segment of the exhibition to view the model of the Agora as it was in the 2nd century A.D., the time of its fullest development (see the *Agora Site Guide*, pp. 22–24).

ROMAN PORTRAITS (1ST–2ND CENTURY A.D.): WEALTHY ATHENIAN CITIZENS REPRESENTED ACCORDING TO THE IMPERIAL PROTOTYPES

As the Roman Empire grew in power and reach, portraits of emperors and their families were disseminated widely. Although these must have imitated individual characteristics to some degree, they functioned propagandistically as portrayals of power and virtue. Representations of local individuals often followed the trends set by Rome—particularly noticeable in features like hairstyle—and depictions of upper-class citizens sent messages about status and merit through a mixture of the old Greek and new imperial vocabularies.

PORTRAIT HEAD, POSSIBLY OF TRAJAN

That the high rank of the subject did not always elicit outstanding quality in a portrait is demonstrated by the first piece in this section of the exhibit, a large head of Pentelic marble wreathed in laurel (S 347). The very generalized expression makes identification difficult, but the head may represent the emperor Trajan (A.D. 98–117). It might be associated with a statue base of Trajan (I 7353) found in the south colonnade of the road leading to the Roman Agora **47**. Other identifications have been suggested: a Flavian priest, Claudius, or Domitian. Like the head of Lucius Aelius Caesar to the visitor's left, the sculpture was found in the ruins of the water mill to the south of the Stoa of Attalos **50**.

T. L. Shear, *AJA* 37 (1933), pp. 308–309; T. L. Shear, *Hesperia* 4 (1935), pp. 411–413; *Agora* I (1953), pp. 27–28, no. 17; G. Hafner, *Späthellenistische Bildnisplastik* (Berlin, 1954), pp. 85–86, no. A 44; *AgPicBk* 5 (1960), fig. 11; C. C. Vermeule, *Roman Imperial Art in Greece and Asia Minor* (Cambridge, Mass., 1968), pp. 387–388; L. A. Riccardi, *Hesperia* 69 (2000), pp. 124–125.

PORTRAIT HEAD, POSSIBLY OF LUCIUS AELIUS VERUS CAESAR

This bearded male portrait head in Pentelic marble and of heroic scale is an outstanding work of the early Antonine period (S 335: 2nd century A.D.). The head has been conjecturally identified as Lucius Aelius Verus Caesar. Adopted by the Emperor Hadrian with a view to becoming his successor, Aelius died too soon (January 1, 138 B.C.); his son, Lucius Verus, however, was later coemperor with Marcus Aurelius. The head was found in the wheel pit of the water mill to the south of the Stoa of Attalos ⑤⓪.

T. L. Shear, *AJA* 37 (1933), p. 309; T. L. Shear, *Hesperia* 4 (1935), pp. 416–418; *Agora* I (1953), pp. 38–41, no. 28; *AgPicBk* 5 (1960), front cover, fig. 13; *Hesperia* Suppl. 22 (1988), p. 81, n. 89.

PORTRAIT BUST OF A YOUNG MAN

The first piece in the next group is a bust of a young man of the early Flavian period, complete but much battered (S 1319: second half of the 1st century A.D.). A tenon for setting it into a base is preserved at the bottom back edge. Short, curly hair and the first flush of a beard are rendered without much detail. The sculptor seems to have drawn on Classical Athenian images of *ephebes* (young men undergoing military service) for this portrait.

H. A. Thompson, *Hesperia* 18 (1949), p. 220; *Agora* I (1953), pp. 25–26, no. 14; *Hesperia* Suppl. 22 (1988), p. 94, n. 23; L. A. Riccardi, *Hesperia* 76 (2007), pp. 379–380.

PORTRAIT HEAD, PROBABLY OF A PRIEST

The middle portrait head, of the Antonine period (S 526: mid-2nd century A.D.), is a very sensitive representation of an elderly man. The rolled headband (*strophion*) indicates that he is probably a priest.

Agora I (1953), p. 41, no. 29.

PORTRAIT HEAD OF A WOMAN, PROBABLY FAUSTINA THE YOUNGER

The cutting at the back of this portrait (S 336: 2nd century A.D.) shows that it was carved separately and attached to the rest of the statue, which included a mantle drawn over the head. That the hair on the right side of the head is only roughly worked suggests that the mantle covered this side more fully. The hairstyle—particularly the waves parted in the center and the spiral curls in front of the ears—is paralleled in portraits of the wife of the emperor Marcus Aurelius, Faustina the Younger (A.D. 145–175). The white marble looks Pentelic but might have been imported from the island of Thasos.

Agora I (1953), pp. 44–45, no. 33.

PORTRAIT HEAD OF A WOMAN

Set in the foreground of the display platform is a portrait of an unidentified woman in very good condition (S 3423). The date is the last quarter of the 2nd century A.D. because of the drilled pupils and hairstyle, particularly the large bun and the curls toward the back on the neck, which often served to indicate a wig. The head was found reused in a Byzantine wall at the north side of the Agora square. It had been placed in the wall upside down with its eyes scratched out, likely by Christian iconoclasts who wanted to cancel its perceived powers.

L. A. Riccardi in *The Athenian Agora: New Perspectives on an Ancient Site* (Mainz, 2009), pp. 55–57.

UNFINISHED PORTRAIT HEADS

Next are three heads, one of a man (S 938) and two of women (S 362, S 1237) of the period 160–180 A.D. All are of Pentelic marble and all are incomplete in varying degrees. The flesh parts of the man's head still show chisel marks that eventually would have been removed by rasping, and the eyeballs have not been incised and drilled as would have been done had the head been finished. One woman's head (S 362) likewise retains chisel work on the face, though the forehead has already been rasped; the iris has not been incised nor the pupil drilled. A close look reveals measuring points on the chin and in the hair to either side of the part. On the second woman's head (S 1237, displayed at the foreground of the platform), the face and neck have been rasped, but the chest is still in a roughly chiseled state. Measuring points remain in the front hair, and masses of marble were never removed from the sides to permit insertion into a socket in the top of the torso.

These and many other pieces of unfinished marble sculpture come from sculptor's workshops, of which traces have been found especially outside the southwest corner of the Agora in the Classical period and around the southeast corner in the Roman period (see p. 31). One unfinished female portrait (S 362) was found in a room in the front of the Library of Pantainos ㊽, which was certainly a sculptor's studio. Of the many indications of technical interest that come from the study of such unfinished work is the observation that in the 2nd century A.D., as shown by the measuring points, portraits were sometimes made with the aid of models.

S 938: *Agora* I (1953), p. 42, no. 30. **S 362**: T. L. Shear, *Hesperia* 4 (1935), pp. 414–416; *Agora* I (1953), pp. 48–49, no. 36; *AgPicBk* 5 (1960), fig. 25; *AgPicBk* 27 (2006), p. 23. **S 1237**: H. A. Thompson, *Hesperia* 17 (1948), p. 179; *Agora* I (1953), pp. 46–47, no. 35; *AgPicBk* 5 (1960), fig. 24.

PORTRAIT HEAD OF A MAN

Displayed facing north at the end of the platform is a male portrait (S 1091: 2nd century A.D.). The short, curly hair and light beard and moustache are consistent with sculpture of the Hadrianic period. Near the front of the head is a series of drill holes into which a metal wreath must have been set. This wreath might indicate that he was a priest.

Agora I (1953), pp. 34–35, no. 24.

HERMS WITH PORTRAITS OF STATE OFFICIALS HONORED BY THE CITY (2ND–3RD CENTURIES A.D.)

Depictions of the god Hermes as a Herm have already been viewed in the ground-floor colonnade (p. 40), and a few more will be seen in the gallery (p. 154). Next in the upstairs gallery is a group of three Herms in which the head is no longer that of a divinity but rather a portrait of a human being. In the Hellenistic and Roman periods, Herms began to be used as a medium for honorary portrait dedications, particularly for officials who represented their Athenian tribe or worked with young men of military age (*ephebes*).

THREE PORTRAIT HERMS

In two of the three Herms in the present group both the head and the shaft have survived—a rare situation. The form was traditional. One reason for its continuing popularity lay in the practical advantages it afforded for displaying a portrait: the shaft supported the head at a convenient height, and at the same time provided space for a dedicatory inscription.

The Herm on the right (S 2056: early 3rd century A.D.) was left unfinished. Note the measuring points on chin and forehead, the rough tooling of the cheeks, and the lack of arm stumps and inscription. The subject had probably served a term as a director of youth training (*kosmetes*) in the early 3rd century A.D., a period when such officials were regularly honored in this way. The Herm was found close to the bust of the "Young Syrian" (S 2062, p. 92).

The middle Herm (Fig. 50; S 586), according to its inscription, represents Moiragenes, son of Dromokles, of the deme of Koile, Eponymous of the tribe Hippothontis. Here the title "eponymous" is used for a patron who provided financial support when it was his tribe's turn to serve as Councilors (*prytaneis*). The modeling and the tentatively incised treatment of the eyes indicate a date in the middle of the 2nd century A.D. during the reign of Hadrian. The top of the head was cut separately and attached with cement.

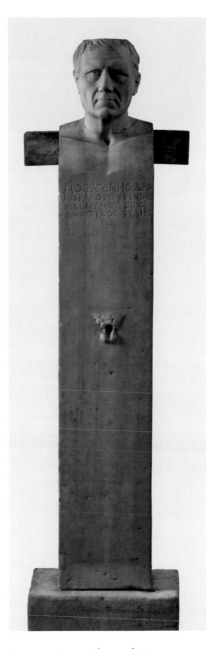

Figure 50. Portrait herm of Moiragenes, mid-2nd century A.D.

This is a lifelike depiction of a typical well-to-do Athenian of the time.

The fragmentary Herm on the left (S 387) with short beard and tousled hair is of the 3rd century A.D. This again represents an important Athenian citizen, perhaps another *kosmetes*.

S 2056: E. B. Harrison, *Hesperia* 29 (1960), pp. 389–390; *AgPicBk* 5 (1960), fig. 30; *Agora* XI (1965), p. 140. **S 586**: T. L. Shear, *Hesperia* 5 (1936), pp. 16–17; *Hesperia* Suppl. 6 (1941), p. 3; *Agora* I (1953), pp. 35–37, no. 25; M. T. Mitsos and E. Vanderpool, *Hesperia* 22 (1953), p. 180; *AgPicBk* 5 (1960), fig. 27; *Agora* XVIII (2011), no. H372. **S 387**: T. L. Shear, *Hesperia* 4 (1935), pp. 419–420; *Agora* I (1953), pp. 52–53, no. 39; *AgPicBk* 5 (1960), fig. 28.

ROMAN PORTRAITS (3RD CENTURY A.D.): PRIVATE AND PROMINENT CITIZENS IN ROMAN ATHENS

The 3rd century A.D. opened with the lingering prosperity initiated by Hadrian's attention toward Greece, but the remainder of the century was marked by the Herulian sack of 267 A.D. and various crises of leadership in the Roman Empire. The names of the individuals represented in these portraits are lost to us, but each one must have been found worthy of commemoration for his involvement in the political, religious, or economic life of the city.

PORTRAIT HEAD WEARING A BUST-CROWN

This over life-size portrait head of white marble probably comes from a full-length draped statue (Fig. 51; S 3500). It is remarkable for the tripartite crown the man wears: the rolled fillet (*strophion*) on the bottom is tied with ribbons (*tainiae*) hanging down at the back, above it is a myrtle wreath, and on top is a band decorated with eight small, individualized busts representing emperors, each wearing military dress. Portraits of men wearing this type of bust-crown are rare in mainland Greece, and this is the only one thus far known from Athens.

The portrait can be dated to the late 2nd–early 3rd century A.D. by the style of the hair and crown. The close-cropped beard of the central bust on the crown (Fig. 52, left) fits the iconography of the emperor Caracalla (ruled A.D. 211–217); if this identification is correct, then the figure at his right wearing the *gorgoneion* is his father, the emperor

Septimius Severus (Fig. 52, right). The contrast between the voluminous, curly hair, carved with a drill, and the schematic, incised beard and rasp marks on the cheeks indicates that the image was later reworked in the mid- to late 3rd century A.D. These changes were probably made in order to reuse the sculpture to represent a different individual, but it is also possible they served to "update" the portrait and give it a more current look.

Bust-crowns were part of the costume of *agonothetai,* officials who directed festival competitions, but were also associated with delegates to the Panhellenion, an institution founded by Hadrian. Its members met in an as yet undiscovered location in Eleusis or Athens and their duties included imperial cult activities and managing the Panhellenia, quadrennial athletic games. The fact that this head was

Figure 51. Portrait of a man wearing a bust-crown, late 2nd–early 3rd century A.D.

discovered in 2002 in the area of the Eleusinion **56** (disposed of in a Byzantine context) and wears a myrtle crown (as do Eleusinian initiates and priests) reflects the close connection between Eleusis and the Panhellenion.

L. A. Riccardi, *Hesperia* 76 (2007) pp. 365–390; J. McK. Camp II, *Hesperia* 76 (2007), pp. 654–655; L. A. Riccardi in *The Athenian Agora: New Perspectives on an Ancient Site* (Mainz, 2009), pp. 58–61.

Figure 52. Figures identified on the bust-crown as possibly Caracalla (left) and Septimius Severus (right)

PORTRAIT HEAD OF A PRIEST

This head (S 564), set on the platform facing west, also portrays an official involved in the religious life of the city. The laurel wreath and shaven head probably mark him as a priest, of the 2nd or 3rd century A.D.

T. L. Shear, *AJA* 39 (1935), pp. 446–447; *Agora* I (1953), pp. 56–57, no. 43; G. Hafner, *Späthellenistische Bildnisplastik* (Berlin, 1954), p. 107; *AgPicBk* 5 (1960), fig. 32.

PORTRAIT HEADS OF BOY INITIATES INTO THE ELEUSINIAN MYSTERIES

Set further back are portrait heads of two young boys of the 3rd century A.D. (S 1312: middle of the 3rd century A.D.; S 1307: first half of the 3rd century A.D.). Both wear wreaths that indicate that they had been initiated into the Eleusinian Mysteries. Both have close-cropped hair, but S 1307 (on the right) has a single long lock falling from the crown to the back of the head; S 1312 might have had a similar lock now broken away. Such locks, according to ancient practice, were reserved for dedication to some divinity after coming of age. These portraits fit the iconography of the hearth-initiate, an honorary position at the Mysteries reserved for a child.

S 1312: H. A. Thompson, *Hesperia* 18 (1949), p. 220; *Agora* I (1953), pp. 60–61, no. 46; *AgPicBk* 5 (1960), fig. 41. **S 1307**: H. A. Thompson, *Hesperia* 17 (1948), p. 179; *Agora* I (1953), pp. 54–55, no. 41; *AgPicBk* 5 (1960), fig. 40. **Both heads**: K. Clinton, *The Sacred Officials of the Eleusinian Mysteries* (1974), pp. 104–108.

PORTRAIT HEADS OF YOUNG MEN

The next two heads, both representing young men, illustrate some of the stylistic differences between the earlier and later 3rd century A.D. The portrait on the right (S 954: A.D. 215–225) sports a light moustache and beard reminiscent of the young emperor Elagabalus (ruled A.D. 218–222); his hair is full, thick, and curly. That on the left is among the latest portraits from the Agora (S 1406: A.D. 250–300). The context of its discovery suggests that the portrait suffered in the Herulian sack, but some of its characteristics point toward the 4th century. The shape and features of this head are more linear, and the stippled beard is impressionistic, not unlike that of the reworking on the bust-crown portrait (S 3500, pp. 88–89).

S 954: *Agora* I (1953), p. 51, no. 38. **S 1406**: H. A. Thompson, *Hesperia* 19 (1950), pp. 331–332; *Agora* I (1953), pp. 65–67, no. 51; *AgPicBk* 5 (1960), fig. 42; L. A. Riccardi, *Hesperia* 76 (2007), p. 379.

FOUR MALE PORTRAIT HEADS

The next four male heads introduce more anonymous Athenians who must have distinguished themselves in the life of the city in their time. The first two (S 517 and S 2434) are of the early 3rd century A.D.: the remarkably large number of good marble portraits of the late 2nd and early 3rd centuries from the Agora excavations is a testimony to the prosperity of the city that followed on the revival in the time of Hadrian. S 517 (A.D. 210–220) probably represents a *kosmetes* and is of the same type as the Herm S 2056 (p. 87). S 2434 wears a heavier beard and a wreath, probably of laurel, a symbol of some honor he received. Next (S 580: ca. A.D. 245–255) is probably another *kosmetes,* this one dated to the middle of the century by his wide-lidded, deeply contoured eyes and coarsely marked forehead wrinkles and hair. The final portrait (S 950: A.D. 253–268), a victim of the Herulian sack, is the latest of the four. The style of the eyes and hair along with flatness of expression conforms to the period of the emperor Gallienus.

S 517: T. L. Shear, *AJA* 39 (1935), pp. 180–181; *Agora* I (1953), pp. 49–50, no. 37; *AgPicBk* 5 (1960), fig. 29; *Hesperia* 76 (2007), pp. 376–377. **S 580**: T. L. Shear, *AJA* 39 (1935), pp. 446–447; *Agora* I (1953), pp. 57–59, no. 44; *AgPicBk* 5 (1960), fig. 34. **S 950**: *Agora* I (1953), pp. 62–63, no. 48.

PORTRAITS WITH NON-GREEK FEATURES

The Roman Empire was large and inclusive, so it is unsurprising to find non-Athenians and even non-Greeks represented in portraiture in and around the Agora. S 435 (3rd century A.D.) shows some "African" features. His young age suggests that he might have been honored as an athletic victor. Next to him is a portrait (S 2445: A.D. 250–275) that achieves a lively effect through the carving of the inner details of the eye and the baroque treatment of the hair. His similarities to

In A.D. 529, the emperor Justinian closed the philosophical schools. The Omega House became a Christian home, and most of its pagan vestiges—including its sculpted decor—were either removed or destroyed.

STATUE OF YOUTHFUL HERMES

First is a well-preserved statue of the god Hermes of about two-thirds life size (S 1054: 2nd century A.D.). As messenger of the gods, Hermes carries the herald's staff (*caduceus*) and wears winged sandals. In his missing right hand he probably held a pouch. He wears a light cloak (*chlamys*), fastened with a now missing brooch (*fibula*) over the right shoulder. The head was made separately and inset. The stump of a palm tree beside the right leg was likely added by the copyist working in marble; the bronze original would not have needed such support. It is a copy of a work of the 4th century B.C., and like the Herakles to the viewer's left (S 2438), it is an excellent example of the facile adaptations of Classical prototypes turned out in great numbers by Athenian sculptors in the Roman period.

This statue of Pentelic marble was found at the level of the 6th century A.D. in a well at the north foot of the Areopagus, probably associated with one of the large houses in the area **57**. Like the sculptures from the Omega House **58**, the Hermes had probably been put out of sight by zealous Christians.

T. L Shear, *Hesperia* 8 (1939), pp. 214, 236, 238; *Agora* XXIV (1988), pp. 41, 46.

STATUE OF A YOUTHFUL HERAKLES

Beside Hermes stands a statue of the youthful Herakles, about two-thirds life size, in Pentelic marble (S 2438: 2nd century A.D.). Over his left forearm is draped the lion skin. In his now-missing left hand he probably held the golden apples of the Hesperides. The right arm is missing below the elbow, but the hand must have rested on the club; its heavy end remains on the plinth. A narrow band encircles the head. The back of the statue and the front of the right foot are only summarily finished.

Probably carved in the 2nd century A.D., this statue is a free adaptation and combination of elements derived from earlier works: the torso has the quality of the first half of the 5th century B.C.; the head is reminiscent of the 4th century. Despite the distressing disproportion of head to body and the evidence of hasty finish, this modest work conveys the vigor of the young hero. The statue was found in 1971 in one of the wells associated with the Omega House . The portrait of Antoninus Pius on the ground floor (S 2436, p. 54) and the two busts of Roman matrons against the north wall (S 2437, S 2435, pp. 97–98) were found in the same well.

T. L. Shear Jr., *Hesperia* 42 (1973), pp. 172–173; O. Palagia, *OJA* 3 (1984), pp. 114–116; J. McK. Camp II, *The Athenian Agora* (London, 1986), pp. 208, 210; *Agora* XXIV (1988), pp. 41, 46.

STATUE OF ASKLEPIOS
Displayed facing north at the end of the platform is a statue of a god (S 1068: possibly 2nd century A.D.), heavily wrapped in a *chiton* and *himation,* leaning on a long staff at his left side. The staff retains a portion of the god's snake companion, indicating that this is Asklepios, the healing god. About one-half life size, it lacks the head and right arm.

Agora XXIV (1988), p. 41.

STATUE OF ATHENA
The small statue of the goddess Athena to the left of Asklepios lacks the head, left arm, and right forearm (S 2337: 2nd century A.D.). It may be restored with a spear in the raised left hand and with some light object such as an offering bowl (*phiale*) in the outstretched right. The left knee is bent. In addition to a sleeved *chiton, peplos,* and aegis, the goddess wears a heavy *himation* neatly folded and fastened at the shoulders in such a way that it falls straight down and covers only her back. Her hair, too, was confined to her back, where it falls in a heavy mass only roughly blocked out. The snakes' heads bordering the aegis were of bronze set in drilled holes. She resembles the Athena Parthenos in some features. Although the sculptural type is of the 4th century B.C., this modest statue was carved in the period of the Antonines. It was later decapitated and reused as a doorstep in the Omega House .

T. L. Shear Jr., *Hesperia* 40 (1971), pp. 274–275; T. L. Shear Jr., *Hesperia* 42 (1973), p. 163; J. McK. Camp II, *The Athenian Agora* (London, 1986), pp. 205, 210; *Agora* XXIV (1988), p. 90; L. J. Roccos, *Hesperia* 60 (1991), pp. 397–410; L. E. Baumer, *Vorbilder und Vorlagen: Studien zur klassischen Frauenstatuen und ihrer Verwendung für Reliefs und Statuetten des 5. und 4. Jahrhunderts von Christus* (Bern, 1997), p. 71, n. 493; *AgPicBk* 27 (2006), p. 51.

 Six sculptures are arranged in a row across the Stoa's north wall. Begin at the left.

BUST OF HELIOS THE SUN GOD

On the far left is displayed another bust (Fig. 49; S 2355: 2nd century A.D.) that is loosely related to the young Alexander viewed previously (Fig. 48; S 2089, pp. 81–82). It is slightly larger than life size and was recovered from a well in the courtyard of the Omega House 58. Here, too, the bust is of unusual shape; it shows only a little of the chest, again with the upper edge of the tunic, and ends abruptly below in a horizontal line. The bust had been damaged and repaired in antiquity: the nose is a replacement and the lips have been reworked. Originally the bust stood out in high relief against a background about 5 cm thick, most of which was trimmed away by the repairers. The back is flat and has a large socket likely for a dowel to secure the bust to a wall.

This second bust appears to be a free adaptation of the same original from which the first was derived. The hair pattern is less rich, the brow protrudes more, and the mouth is shorter. In place of a continuous headband, this bust has a row of 15 drilled holes evenly spaced over the skull. These must have held metal spikes forming a radiate crown that would have stood out against the original background. Therefore, the figure can be identified as Helios the sun god, whose iconography for centuries ran parallel with that of Alexander, the two interacting one with the other. This Helios was probably carved in the 2nd century A.D. and damaged in the sack by the Herulians in A.D. 267 before being brought to the Omega House.

T. L. Shear Jr., *Hesperia* 40 (1971), pp. 273–274; J. McK. Camp II, *The Athenian Agora* (London, 1986), p. 204; *Agora* XXIV (1988), pp. 37, 41.

HEAD OF A GODDESS, PROBABLY NEMESIS

This representation of a goddess (S 1055: 1st century A.D.) features abundant wavy hair held firmly by a high diadem, the upper edge of which is broken in such a way as to indicate that it was interrupted at intervals by projecting knobs. The head has been identified as coming from a much-reduced copy, carved in the Early Roman period, of the cult image of Nemesis made for her temple at Rhamnous by Agorakritos ca. 435–430 B.C. It was found in the same well as the Hermes (S 1054, p. 94).

T. L. Shear, *Hesperia* 8 (1939), pp. 214, 240, 241; G. Despinis, Συμβολή στη μελέτη του έργου του Αγορακρίτου (Athens, 1971), p. 78, n. 153; *Agora* XXIV (1988), p. 41.

PORTRAIT BUSTS OF ROMAN MATRONS

Next are displayed two well-preserved, high-quality busts of otherwise unknown Athenian women. They were found together in a well in the Omega House 58. The bust to the left (Fig. 55; S 2435: 3rd century A.D.) has retained its square, profiled pedestal; the other (S 2437: 2nd century A.D.) lacks its base. In both cases the bust is of a shape standard in the 2nd and early 3rd centuries A.D., in which both *chiton* and *himation* are rendered in full detail. The best clue to the dating is provided by comparison of the coiffure with those on imperial portraits. This yields a date in

Figure 55. *Portrait bust of a woman, 3rd century A.D.*

the last quarter of the 2nd century for S 2437 (right), whose hair is swept back from the brow and wrapped in a coiled braid around the back of the head. On S 2435 (left), the hair is combed down over the ears but also coiled above the back of the head, a fashion best paralleled in the early 3rd century. S 2435 also wears a heavy rolled headband tied at the back, and above it an olive wreath, perhaps marking her as a priestess of Athena.

Both portraits: T. L. Shear Jr., *Hesperia* 42 (1973), pp. 171–172; J. McK. Camp II, *The Athenian Agora* (London, 1986), pp. 208–209; *Agora* XXIV (1988), p. 41. **S 2435:** *AgPicBk* 27 (2006), p. 52.

PORTRAIT HEAD OF A MAN
This portrait of the Antonine period (S 2356: 2nd century A.D.) was discovered in the same well as the Helios bust (S 2355, p. 96). The man is middle-aged and depicted with a furrowed brow. Only the lower parts of his ears are visible under his ample, curly hair. The hair and bushy beard were carved using a drill, while the skin is highly polished; this variation results in a skillful interplay of light and shadow.

T. L. Shear Jr., *Hesperia* 40 (1971), p. 274; J. McK. Camp II, *The Athenian Agora* (London, 1986), p. 204; *Agora* XXIV (1988), p. 41; *AgPicBk* 27 (2006), p. 30.

HERM IN THE FORM OF A DROWSY SILENOS
At the right end of the row stands a life size figure heavily draped in a sleeved and belted *chiton* with the end of a cloak slung over the left shoulder (Fig. 56; S 2363: 2nd century A.D.). His head is encircled by a sausage-like wreath bound spirally with a ribbon. He wears a shaggy beard; his expression is drowsy, sly, and sardonic. With his left hand he plucks his clothing; in his right hand, now broken away, he held some object of which only traces remain. The figure terminates below in a downward tapering shaft that is part of a broader pier continuing up the back and curving forward over the head: the shape is similar to that of a Herm. The figure evidently served as a fence-post in the Omega House 58, and probably had a companion piece. Despite the unusual dress the figure is probably Silenos, but he has similarities to contemporary figures of Dionysos and Priapos.

Agora XXIV (1988), p. 41.

Figure 56. Draped herm of a drowsy Silenos, 2nd century A.D.

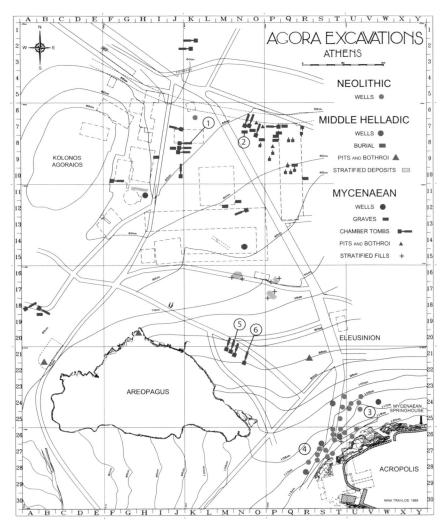

Figure 57. Plan of the Agora area showing Neolithic and Bronze Age wells and graves (ca. 3200–1100 B.C.)

CASE 1. NEOLITHIC FIGURINE

In the central freestanding case is a marble figurine of a reclining woman (photo p. 10, top left; S 1097) whose chest is turned perpendicular to her hips; the head is missing. Dating from the end of the Middle Neolithic period, this is one of the earliest pieces of stone

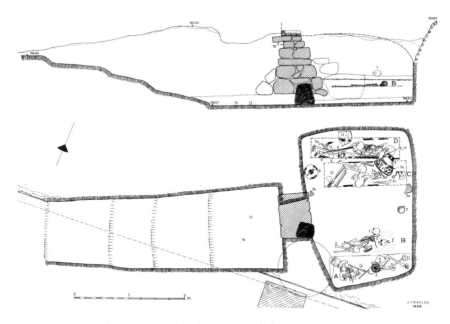

Figure 58. A typical Mycenaean chamber tomb, with four separate burials

sculpture known from Athens. It has close affinities with still earlier statuettes in Anatolia. The figurine was found in an unstratified context in the area of the Eleusinion **56**.

CASE 81. POTTERY FROM LATE NEOLITHIC THROUGH EARLY BRONZE AGE WELLS

The two plump jars of red burnished ware on the bottom shelf (P 14871, P 14872) are among the earliest complete vases known from Athens; they date from the end of the Late Neolithic period, ca. 3000 B.C., and come from a series of 20 early wells on the northwest slope of the Acropolis (Fig. 57:3). A number of sherds from the same source (nos. 1–12) are mounted on the wall above to illustrate some of the finer fabrics of this period: red and black, burnished, and incised, all shaped by hand (i.e., not wheelmade).

The Early Bronze Age, designated for mainland Greece as Early Helladic and dated ca. 3000–2000 B.C., is very sparsely represented in the Agora. A few characteristic sherds (nos. 13–17) have been laid out on the top row of the lower wall hanging. They show that many of the old ceramic techniques persisted from the Neolithic period: burnishing, incising, and mottling. Among the innovations is the use of a very thin, dull paint (Urfirnis) on which simple geometric designs can be overpainted (no. 16; P 13957). Among the most characteristic shapes of the period are the bowl with incurved rim at the upper left (no. 13; P 27031) and the sauceboat with cream-colored paint at the upper right (no. 17; P 14844).

For the Middle Helladic period (ca. 2000–1550 B.C.) the material is more abundant. Most of it, again, comes from wells (Fig. 57:4), five of them on the northwest slope of the Acropolis, but domestic deposits of the period have been found also on the lower slopes of the Areopagus and beneath the Royal Stoa ㉖, while a sprinkling of sherds of this period has been observed over much of the area. The bottom row of the lower wall display (nos. 18–20) contains specimens of the most characteristic wares of the time: Matte-painted and Gray Minyan, in addition to another burnished bowl (P 10743, P 9733, P 10533).

CASE 80. POTTERY AND VARIOUS OBJECTS FROM WELLS, EARLY–MIDDLE BRONZE AGE

This case continues the examination of Early and Middle Bronze Age (late 3rd millennium–1600 B.C.) material with an exhibition of whole pieces and non-pottery objects. Of the Middle Bronze pottery, note especially the Gray Minyan two-handled cup on the top shelf (no. 7; P 13968), perhaps an imitation of silver. In the Matte-painted vases simple geometric designs have been rendered in dull black paint on a light ground. Especially pleasing is the two-handled spouted bowl also on the top shelf (no. 4; P 10521). The long-spouted, one-handled bowl on the bottom shelf was decorated in white against the red ground of the clay (no. 2; P 10522). In shape both of these vessels show the influence of Minoan Crete.

Of the nonceramic material on the bottom shelf, note particularly objects of everyday use, such as a spindle whorl for working wool into yarn (no. 6; MC 527), stone tools, blades of stone and obsidian, and a worked, pierced horn of uncertain use (no. 9; BI 409).

CASES 79 AND 78. POTTERY FROM MYCENAEAN CHAMBER TOMBS

Cases 79 and 78 present some of the characteristic ceramic material of the Mycenaeans (15th–12th centuries B.C.). In Case 79, the two-handled goblet on the top shelf (left) in both shape and color is an imitation of a gold vase (no. 1; P 21262). The two large wine pitchers on the bottom left (nos. 1 and 2; P 23578, P 23587) with their strap handles and trough spouts also show the influence of metalwork, in this case bronze. Above, in the center, is a third pitcher of similar form on which an octopus has been applied with great feeling for its decorative possibilities (no. 3; P 21246). Next to it, the two-handled open bowl (no. 4; P 21200), with the fish and duck swimming ceaselessly round the margin of the pool (Fig. 59), and the large one-handled mug (no. 5; P 19211) are shown by their thick walls and coarse workmanship to be among the latest Mycenaean (Late Helladic IIIC).

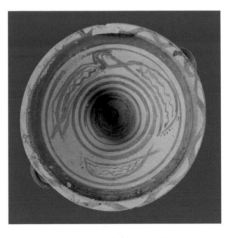

Figure 59. A fish and duck "swim" on the interior of a Mycenaean bowl

In Case 78, the large mixing bowl of ca. 1375–1350 B.C., set on the stump of ancient Stoa wall (no. 1; P 21564) is decorated in an unusually delicate pictorial style; in the middle of its wall is a horned altar on which stood a double axe. On the shelf in front are several vases of the standard shapes and decoration of this period, including a *kylix* (drinking cup) preserving part of a painted octopus (photo p.10, bottom left; no. 1; P 21591).

CASE 1. MINIATURE VASES AND FIGURINES FROM CHILDREN'S TOMBS OF THE MYCENAEAN PERIOD

In a small display at the rear of the central case sits a group of characteristic offerings from children's graves of the 14th–13th centuries B.C. The six vases are miniature and include a spouted feeding bottle (no. 3; P 23726) and a funnel (no. 1; P 23696). The terracotta figurines (nos. 4–6) with their highly schematic shapes were also commonly placed in children's tombs, perhaps as playthings or symbolic nurses for the journey to the other world.

CASES 7–9. OFFERINGS FROM A MYCENAEAN CHAMBER TOMB OF A RICH ATHENIAN LADY

Return to the start of the exhibit and walk along the right wall. The first three cases on this side are devoted to another chamber tomb on the Areopagus (see Fig. 57:6 in the *Agora Site Guide*, p. 147; Late Helladic IIIA, ca. 1400).

In Case 8 a model shows the rectangular tomb chamber bordered to right and left by benches for offerings; in one corner is the burial pit with its stone lid. The doorway had been walled up after funeral services, and was discovered in this condition. The burial pit had been opened, however, and the body removed, presumably in consequence of the collapse of the roof. The offerings comprised eight vases of various shapes, several ivory hairpins, a bronze mirror, a long-handled copper lamp, and two ivory jewel boxes. Familiar shroud ornaments consisting of thin gold plates of various shapes, all pierced for stitching, were found on the floor of the tomb and in the burial pit.

Noteworthy among the offerings are the two ivory boxes, both richly carved in low relief (Case 9, top shelf). On the wall and the lid of the larger box (no. 3; BI 511) griffins pull down deer (Fig. 60); the smaller box (no. 2; BI 513) has a nautilus design. These boxes rank among the finest known examples of Mycenaean ivory carving. The ivory was imported from Egypt or Syria.

A witness to foreign trade found in this tomb is the large pointed *amphora* of coarse reddish clay exhibited in Case 7 (no. 2; P 15358). This jar is of a type known to have been made in Canaan and exported widely around the eastern Mediterranean. It presumably contained some product of the land where it was made, e.g., incense, myrrh, or spices.

As the largest and most richly furnished burial place of the Mycenaean period yet found in Athens, the chamber tomb on the Areopagus must be assigned to one of the principal Athenian families of the period.

General: T. L. Shear, *Hesperia* 9 (1940), pp. 274–291; *Agora* XIII (1971), pp. 158–169. **Canaanite jar**: V. R. Grace in *The Aegean and the Near East* (Locust Valley, New York, 1956), pp. 80–109.

Figure 60. Ivory pyxis *with griffins attacking deer, late 15th century* B.C., *photograph and watercolor*

CASES 10 AND 11. OFFERINGS FROM OTHER MYCENAEAN TOMBS

On the top shelf of Case 10 are ceramic offerings from a pit grave of an infant girl of Late Helladic IIB date (ca. 1400 B.C.) located to the west of the Stoa of Attalos (Fig. 57:2). Here again the vases are for the most part small, in keeping with the tender years of the deceased. Particularly pleasing in this group is the bowl on the far right with lilies on its wall and with three suspension loops on its rim (no. 10; P 21300).

The bottom shelf of Case 10 and the whole of Case 11 contain the furnishings of a chamber tomb on the Areopagus (Fig. 57:5). Three burials had been made in the tomb in fairly rapid succession within the Late Helladic IIIA period (first half of the 14th century b.c.). The latest burial was that of a young man. On a blue painted table at his side were laid his sword (Case 11 bottom, no. 4; B 778), dagger (no. 2; B 781) and razor (no. 3; B 782), all of bronze. The sword is a good example of the developed Mycenaean type, its narrow blade strengthened with a prominent midrib, the shoulders projecting in long horns. The wooden hilt has vanished leaving only the gold-headed bronze rivets by which it was fastened (no. 10; B 779). On the floor of the tomb lay also a number of beads of steatite, and gold rosettes pierced for stitching to the shroud. On the plain vases of the top shelf of Case 11 (nos. 1–3) are traces of the coating of tin by which they were covered. These vessels were presumably intended for the grave and were so treated to make them look like silver.

CASE 12. MORE MYCENAEAN MATERIAL

In the foreground of this case lies jewelry from a disturbed chamber tomb, just to the south of the Temple of Ares ❸❽ (Fig. 57:1), Late Helladic IIIA in date (14th century b.c.). On the gold ring (no. 2; J 5) a male figure with staff in hand leads two long-skirted female figures rapidly to the right (Fig. 61). In the field above is a small flying figure; on the extreme left is a column-like object. No convincing interpretation has yet been proposed for this vivid little scene.

Figure 61. Mycenaean ring

Behind the jewelry is the lone object not from a tomb: a Late Mycenaean *amphora* (AP 2577, ca. 1200 b.c.) recovered from the underground fountain on the north slope of the Acropolis, a plan of which can be seen on the wall behind.

BURIALS

Most of the artifacts representing the Agora's early history come from burials. One might be surprised to see tombs in this part of Athens. In later periods, burial was generally limited to the area outside the city walls and the Agora was the administrative and commercial center of the city. The chronological pattern fits the claim of the historian Thucydides (2.15.3) that the occupation of very early Athens was centered on the Acropolis and the area to its south. After the Agora was marked as public space, the early tombs were sometimes disturbed by new construction. For example, in the Classical period, workers who came upon a Mycenaean chamber tomb under the Temple of Ares **38** left gifts of *lekythoi* (oil-filled jars) to excuse their transgression. Other tombs were incorporated into the new landscape. A small cemetery south of the Tholos **6** was set up as a *heroon* (hero shrine) and likely had ancestral significance.

Figure 62. Watercolor reconstruction of the funerary bier and chariot race on a Geometric amphora, ca. 725–700 B.C.

The tombs in the Agora reveal how changing social conventions affected burial forms. In the Late Bronze Age there is a tendency toward communal tombs and inhumation, especially in the chamber tombs with their reusable entrances (*dromoi*). Cremation, in turn, dominated the Iron

Age. The building of a pyre for the cremation of Achilles' friend Patroclus, the accompanying sacrifice of animals, and the subsequent funerary games in his honor are famously described in Book 23 of the *Iliad* (Fig. 62; P 4990, p. 109, illustrates such a funeral). The age or gender of the deceased might also be taken into account, as the burial of an infant in a *pithos* shows (Case 72, p. 123).

Figure 63. *Facial reconstruction of a rich Athenian lady, wearing the gold earrings buried with her.*

A variety of gifts were buried with the dead. Many of the vessels were actually containers for offerings of oil, water, or food. Personal items were also common; in the case of cremation, accessories like the intricate gold and glass jewelry of the wealthy woman of Cases 16–17 (pp. 114–116) would be removed beforehand and then reunited with the person's ashes. Because the living members of a family performed the funeral, the choices could also reflect living concerns. For example, the horses atop many of the *pyxides* communicated the wealth and status of the deceased and her family to anyone viewing the funeral (e.g., Case 2, p. 117).

The skeletal material is also instructive. Animal bones reveal that communal meals sometimes occurred near the grave or that sacrificial offerings were made. The examination of human remains can provide information about both the individual (diet, health, age, reason for death) and the population (demography, migration, genetics). In the case of the wealthy woman of the Geometric period, a facial reconstruction was even possible (Fig. 63).

E. D. Townsend, *Hesperia* 24 (1955), pp. 187–219; *AgPicBk* 13 (1973); *Hesperia* Suppl. 43 (2009).

EARLY IRON AGE
(CA. 1100–700 B.C.)

After the collapse of the Bronze Age palace system, Athens and the rest of Greece fell into decline, although the period is also marked by the new, widespread use of iron. The material for the study of this period also comes chiefly from graves, though the grave goods are supplemented in a steadily rising proportion by objects of household use from wells (Fig. 64). Most abundant is the pottery.

Toward the end of the Bronze Age (12th and early 11th centuries B.C.), the craft of the potter had declined: the fabrics became coarse, the shapes lifeless, and the decoration was reduced to the simplest linear patterns. In the latter part of the 11th century a revival set in. The potter took greater pains in preparing clay and gloss, put new life into some of the traditional shapes, devised new shapes, and achieved crisper outlines and more pleasing proportions. A pivoted multiple brush was devised for drawing the groups of concentric circles and semicircles that previously had been done freehand. A few new decorative motifs were introduced: checkerboard, hatched panels, sawtooth, and narrow bands effectively grouped. The early phase of the new movement (ca. 1050–900 B.C.) is known as the Protogeometric period because of the incipient fashion for geometric designs.

The increasing predilection for the geometric was marked by the introduction in about 900 B.C. of the meander pattern and the swastika. Geometric patterns maintained their popularity over the next two centuries. The individual motifs were refined over time, and gradually a logical syntax of decoration evolved. Both the individual motifs and their combinations were clearly borrowed by vase painters from basket makers. Some of the most common vase shapes of the period were also derived from basketry, e.g., the pointed and flat *pyxis* (box) and the hemispherical bowl. Birds and animals were now occasionally admitted in a geometricized form. On vases made for the grave funeral rites began to be represented. Battles on land and sea were occasionally depicted. Finally, specific incidents from mythology were shown in a recognizable form. This marked the beginning of the humanistic and narrative tendencies which were to characterize Greek art of the Classical period. These developments occurred within the so-called Geometric period (9th and 8th centuries B.C.).

bits. The bits, extremely rare in Greek lands, find their best parallels in central Europe.

C. W. Blegen, *Hesperia* 21 (1952), pp. 279–294; *AgPicBk* 13 (1973), figs. 38, 39; J. McK. Camp II, *The Athenian Agora* (London, 1986), pp. 31–32; *AgPicBk* 24 (1998), pp. 10–11.

CASES 16–17. FINDS FROM AN EARLY GEOMETRIC CREMATION BURIAL OF A PREGNANT WEALTHY WOMAN

All the material in these cases comes from the grave of a wealthy woman who died at about the age of 30 in the middle of the 9th century B.C. (Fig. 63). The grave was excavated in 1967 at the northwest foot of the Areopagus (Figs. 64:9, 66; see also the *Agora Site Guide*, p. 147). In Case 17, the Early Geometric *amphora* on the left held the ashes of the body of both the woman and her unborn child, which had been burned on the spot. The woman's more precious jewelry had also been deposited in the *amphora* and was untouched by the fire. The large vase was closed with a mug and placed in a pit in the bedrock. Around its shoulder were heaped a number of vases in fresh condition. The mouth of the pit was closed with a large brick. Among the ashes around the pit were many fragmentary vases and terracotta beads that had been thrown onto the pyre. Animal bones were also collected and placed with the bodies and indicate that a large funeral meal was held by the mourners.

The medium-size *amphora* on the bottom shelf, found with a mug in its mouth (see drawing to right in display case), stood near the great urn. Note the very delicate geometric decoration on the smaller vases. The small open-work vessel is a miniature wool basket. More remarkable is the terracotta model of a linen chest surmounted by a row of five top-shaped granaries, each with a trapdoor near its peak and a pair of holes at its base, perhaps for securing a wooden ladder (Fig. 67). The symbolism communicates an abundance of food and household furnishings, whether in this world or the next.

The jewelry was remarkable for its period in both quantity and quality. The large terracotta beads, which were probably designed for funerary use, had gone through the fire. The unburned jewelry deposited in the urn included four long bronze pins, two bronze fibulae, and a bronze ring (not exhibited). From the urn came also

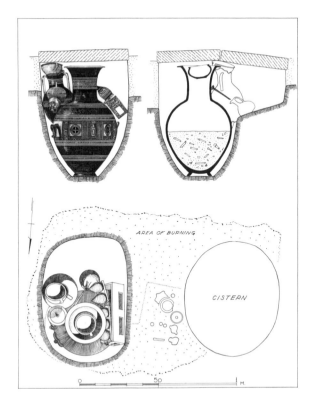

Figure 66. Cremation burial of a wealthy Athenian woman, ca. 850 B.C.

Figure 67. Pyxis with model granaries on lid, ca. 850 B.C.

the glass paste necklace with the banded glass pendant. The gold jewelry discovered in the urn includes three narrow rings, three broad hoops with geometric ornament, and a pair of massive earrings, each comprising a trapezoidal plate with filigree and granular ornament and three pendants in the form of pomegranates (Figs. 63, 68).

Noteworthy also is the small pyramidal seal of ivory, the attribute of a responsible manager of the household.

Figure 68. Gold earring, ca. 850 B.C. (front and back)

E. L. Smithson, *Hesperia* 37 (1968), pp. 77–116; *AgPicBk* 13 (1973), figs. 40–49; J. McK. Camp II, *The Athenian Agora* (London, 1986), pp. 30–31; A. Cherici, *RendLinc* 44 (1989), pp. 215–230; J. N. Coldstream, *Hesperia* 64 (1995), pp. 391–403; *Hesperia* Suppl. 33 (2004), pp. 225–242; M. A. Liston and J. K. Papadopoulos, *Hesperia* 73 (2004), pp. 7–38.

CASES 18–19. POTTERY FROM PROTOGEOMETRIC BURIALS

Cases 18 and 19 display characteristic grave furnishings of the 10th century B.C.: the large vessels (amphoras and hydrias) held the ashes of the cremated body. The offerings were chiefly wine pitchers, drinking cups, and oil flasks such as the deceased would have used in this world and might be expected to need on the journey to the next. Note also the infant's feeding bottle with spout (Case 19, top shelf, no. 4; P 6836).

CASE 20. OFFERINGS FROM AN EARLY GEOMETRIC CREMATION BURIAL OF A WOMAN

Displayed here are the offerings from a woman's grave of ca. 900 B.C. found at the northwest foot of the Areopagus (Fig. 64:6). Generous provision was made by the family for her journey to the other world: eight vases of assorted shapes, a terracotta spindle whorl, earrings probably of electrum (an alloy of gold and silver), and two pairs of heavy traveling boots modeled in clay.

R. S. Young, *Hesperia* 19 (1949), pp. 275–297.

CASES 21–22. OFFERINGS FROM A LATE GEOMETRIC INHUMATION BURIAL OF A WOMAN

These cases contain the offerings from a richly furnished adult burial of the fully developed Geometric period. The burial is of the mid-8th century B.C., and belonged to a family burial plot south of the Tholos ⑥ (Fig. 64:4). In the period between the burial in Case 20 and this one, cremation was abandoned. As then became common for adult burials of this period, the corpse was laid on the floor of a pit cut down into the bedrock. The offerings were placed on or beside the body, and the grave was then covered with rough stone slabs (the grave is illustrated on the back wall of Case 22).

Prominent among the offerings are lidded boxes of terracotta (*pyxides*). They are of the flat variety, perhaps patterned after baskets; the handles on the lids are knob-shaped, or, occasionally, in the form of horses, perhaps already a symbol of a noble status in life and of a heroic status after death. The use of *pyxides* is restricted to graves. They presumably held food offerings to supplement the drink offerings attested by the wine jugs and drinking cups also found in burials of the period.

Hesperia Suppl. 2 (1939), pp. 76–87; *AgPicBk* 24 (1998), p. 10, fig. 16 (*pyxis* with horses, P 5060).

CASE 2. LATE GEOMETRIC *PYXIS* AND *OINOCHOE*

Backtrack to the central case that marks the beginning of the Geometric section. At the back of this case is yet another *pyxis* (ca. 725–700 B.C.) with a handle in the shape of horses (P 4784), about 20–50 years later than those in the previous display.

Around the front of the case is a wine jug (*oinochoe*) decorated with a battle scene (Fig. 69; P 4885: ca. 750–725 B.C.). This piece is interesting for both its structure and its decoration. Two tubes were inserted transversely through the body of the vase. The most probable explanation of this curious arrangement, otherwise unknown, is that it was a device for cooling the contents. When the jug, full of wine, was set in a basin of cold water or let down into a well the water would circulate through the tubes, and thus cool the wine more quickly. It is also possible that it was a trick vase: it could be filled and poured from, even though it appeared to have holes in it.

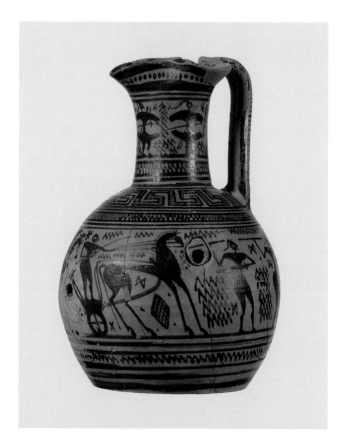

Figure 69. Oinochoe *with battle scenes, ca. 750–725* B.C., *photograph and watercolor*

The vase is decorated with battle scenes: in a band around the body men fight on foot and from chariots; on the neck is a file of heavily armed men. Note the plumed helmet and the figure-eight shield, the long, heavy sword, and the pair of spears. The weapons and the method of fighting are those described by Homer. It has been conjectured, indeed, that the scene represents a particular incident described in the *Iliad* (11.670–761), viz., the fight between the people of Pylos and the Epeians, among whom were twin brothers, sons of Molione, who share the great square shield below the handle of the vase. The identification of the double figure is not without controversy, but if its interpretation as the Homeric twins is correct, this scene would rank among the earliest representations in Greek art of a specific incident.

Pyxis: *Hesperia* Suppl. 2 (1939), pp. 87–93; J. McK. Camp II, *The Athenian Agora* (London, 1986), pp. 31–32; J. K. Papadopoulos in *The Art of Antiquity* (Athens, 2007), pp. 125–128, fig. 120:F, G. **Oinochoe:** R. Hampe, *Frühe griechische Sagenbilder* (Athens, 1936), pp. 87–88; *Hesperia* Suppl. 2 (1939), pp. 68–71; *Agora* XIV (1972), p. 15; J. McK. Camp II, *The Athenian Agora* (London, 1986), pp. 32–33; *AgPicBk* 24 (1998), pp. 9–10, 14; J. K. Papadopoulos in *The Art of Antiquity* (Athens, 2007), pp. 122–123; M. K. Dahm, *Hesperia* 76 (2007), pp. 717–730.

CASE 77. TRIAL PIECES FROM A POTTER'S DUMP

Continue down the left side of the exhibit, beginning with the only case containing objects from this period which are not associated with burials. It contains waste from a potter's workshop of the Early Protogeometric period (ca. 1000 B.C.) recovered from a well beneath the middle of the Agora (Fig. 64:3). This is the earliest evidence for the making of pottery in the district that came to be known as the "Potter's Quarter" (Kerameikos). The fragments shown are trial pieces: bits of pottery daubed with paint which were placed in the kiln along with the whole pots and then pulled out at intervals to enable the potter to check the progress of the firing.

M. C. Monaco, *Ergasteria: impianti artigianali ceramici* (Rome, 2000), pp. 17–24; *Hesperia* Suppl. 31 (2003), pp. 23–189.

Figure 72. Vase in the form of a kneeling boy, ca. 540–530 B.C.

Three fine pieces of Protoattic pottery are displayed at the back. The lion's head on the wine jug (*olpe*) is a striking example of eastern influence (no. 1; P 22550).

Athlete: E. Vanderpool, *Hesperia* 6 (1937), pp. 426–441; *AgPicBk* 3 (1959), fig. 23; G. M. A. Richter, *Kouroi* (London, 1970, 3rd edition), pp. 77–78; *Agora* XIV (1972), p. 186; *AgPicBk* 25 (2003), pp. 30–31; J. K. Papadopoulos et al. in *The Art of Antiquity* (Athens, 2007), pp. 160–161.

CASE 70. POTTERY FROM WELLS

Case 70 on the left, like Case 26 opposite, contains representative objects from the filling of several wells in the 7th century. The imports include an *alabastron* from Corinth (top shelf, no. 5; P 23425) and a lamp from Asia Minor (bottom, no. 7; L 5101), while the pair of horses on the *amphora* (bottom, no. 6; P 22551) was probably inspired by imports from the Greek islands. Also on the bottom shelf, the woman's head painted in outline on the fragmentary *amphora* (no. 3; P 17393) has the boldness of conception and the sure rendering that mark contemporary Attic sculpture, the first monumental statues in marble. A fragment from a large vase preserving two pair of human legs (no. 1; P 576) is Argive; it comes from the debris of a sanctuary. The two-handled cup (*kantharos*) (top shelf, no. 6; P 7014) bears the owner's name painted by the maker on the rim: "I belong to [- - -]ylos."

CASE 69. ARCHAIC SCULPTURE

The final cases devoted to the Archaic period, set perpendicular to the wall on either side of the gallery, both present sculpture. In Case 69, the small head of Herakles wearing the scalp of the Nemean lion as a helmet (no. 1; S 1295) was found in a Late Antique context to the southwest of the Agora. The figure probably adorned a temple that might have stood in that district, Melite, in which was a famous sanctuary of Herakles. The piece is both charming and intriguing. Most elements of the style can be traced to the beginning of the 5th century B.C., but the treatment of the eyes and mouth, and the use of Pentelic rather than island marble, call for a date perhaps in the later part of that century.

The life-size (female?) head of island marble (no. 2; S 1071) was found in a Late Antique context above the Eleusinion **56**; it probably comes from a statue of a maiden (*kore*) dedicated on the Acropolis. The hair is held by a diadem. In front are bangs ending in a double row of snail-shell curls; behind are long, crimped tresses. She wears large disc earrings. The Late Archaic style points to a date at the beginning of the 5th century B.C.

The small (female?) head of Parian marble close to life size (no. 3; S 2476) was found in the Crossroads Enclosure **27** in a context of the late 5th century B.C. (photo p. 10, top center). The face is boldly modeled, the eyeballs bulge, and the crinkly hair is confined by a diadem, which allows a mass to fall down behind while three locks fall over either shoulder in front. She wears disc earrings. The sculptural style of this head, which finds close parallels on the Athenian Treasury at Delphi, points to a date in the early years of the 5th century B.C.

The small inscribed fragment (I 3872 = *IG* I³ 502) comes from the base of the statues of Harmodios and Aristogeiton, who killed Hipparchos, son of the tyrant Peisistratos, in 514 B.C. (see the *Agora Site Guide,* pp. 104–105). The first part of the epigram, which is preserved in the work of a later Greek grammarian, reads:

> *A great light shone for the Athenians when Harmodios*
> *and Aristogeiton slew Hipparchos.*

Part of the name of Harmodios can be discerned. The piece was found in the northern part of the Agora, where Pausanias saw the statues in the 2nd century A.D., and not far from the spot where the deed occurred.

Herakles: *Agora* XI (1965), pp. 37–40, no. 97 A. **Kore**: T. L. Shear, *Hesperia* 8 (1939), pp. 235–237; *Agora* XI (1965), pp. 20–21, no. 73. **Female head**: T. L. Shear Jr., *Hesperia* 42 (1973), pp. 400–401. **Tyrannicide base**: B. D. Meritt, *Hesperia* 5 (1936) pp. 355–358; S. Brunnsåker, *The Tyrant-Slayers of Kritios and Nesiotes* (Lund, 1955); *AgPicBk* 10 (1966), fig. 4; *Agora* III (1957; reprinted 1973), no. 280; *Agora* XIV (1972), pp. 156–157; M. W. Taylor, *The Tyrant Slayers* (2nd edition, Salem, N.H., 1991), pp. 16–18, 32–33.

CASE 27. TERRACOTTA MOLD FOR A BRONZE STATUE

The mold for making a bronze statue of Apollo (S 741) was assembled from debris found in a pit at the west edge of the Agora, just to the south of the Temple of Apollo ㉓. The casting was done by the lost-wax process. In this process, a core of clay was covered by a layer of wax, which was then enveloped in an outer mold built up of three successive layers of clay. After metal skewers were inserted to keep core and mold in their proper relative positions, the wax was melted out. The mold was planted upright in a pit in the bedrock and packed firmly with earth (Fig. 73). Bronze brought to the melting point in a nearby furnace above was poured through a funnel-like opening at the top. On cooling, the mold was stripped away. The parts of the statue that were molded separately were joined, the surface of the bronze was smoothed, and the completed statue was likely set up in

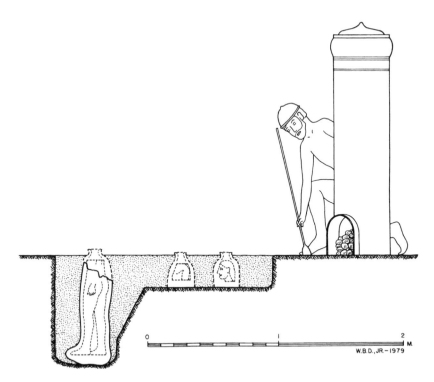

Figure 73. Bronze casting pit and furnace

the nearby temple. Dating from the middle of the 6th century B.C., this mold illustrates the effective simplicity of technical procedure at a time when Greek artists were just beginning to cast statues of hollow bronze.

Fragmentary molds and casting pits for the making of statues datable to the 5th, 4th, and 2nd centuries B.C., and to the 5th century A.D., have been found elsewhere in the excavations (see the *Agora Site Guide,* p. 181).

H. A. Thompson, *Hesperia* 6 (1937), pp. 82–83; *Agora* XIV (1972), pp. 188–190; C. C. Mattusch, *Hesperia* 46 (1977), pp. 340–347; *AgPicBk* 20 (1982), pp. 11–16; C. W. Hedrick Jr., *AJA* 92 (1988), pp. 190–191; C. C. Mattusch, *Greek Bronze Statuary* (Ithaca, 1988), pp. 54–59.

CLASSICAL PERIOD
(480–323 B.C.)

The event that separates the Archaic Period from the Classical is the destruction of Athens by the Persians in 480 B.C. This disaster and the subsequent Athenian victory over the invaders created both the necessity and opportunity for the city to undertake new building projects. This growth can be seen in the Agora especially in the infrastructure and bureaucracy of democracy and commerce.

This section of the gallery is arranged more thematically than chronologically. The excavation has yielded many objects associated with the various departments of civic life that were centered in the Agora: legislation, administration, the judiciary, finance, war memorials, etc. Most of this material dates from the great period of Athens, the late 6th to the late 4th century B.C., and constitutes a valuable supplement to the ancient authors. As these objects are unique to the Agora and illustrate the functioning of the Athenian state, they make up the most important part of the museum collection.

In addition to this civic material, several cases contain pottery of the time and the final case displays coins.

Agora XIV (1972); J. McK. Camp II, *The Athenian Agora* (London, 1986), pp. 61–152; J. Ober and C. W. Hedrick, *The Birth of Democracy* (Athens, 1993); *AgPicBk* 4 (revised 2004).

CASE 28. INSCRIPTIONS ON MARBLE

The Agora, as the most frequented part of the city, was the most common place for setting up inscriptions that were meant to be read by many people. The excavations have yielded over 7,000 inscriptions on marble. A few pieces of outstanding interest are displayed in the first case on the right.

On the bottom shelf (no. 1) is a fragment from the heading of the tribute list of the Athenian Empire for the year 418/7 B.C. (I 4809 = *IG* I³ 287). The greater part of these lists are found in the Epigraphical Museum in Athens. At the lower right of the fragment begins the entry of the amounts paid into the treasury of the goddess Athena from the tribute collected from the region of the Hellespont.

Figure 74. Library rules, ca. A.D. *100*

Next (no. 2) is a fragment from a list of the magistrates, the eponymous archons, who gave their names to the Athenian years (I 4120 = *IG* I³ 1031a). The names preserved here, dating from 527/6 to 522/1 B.C., are [. .]eto[- - -], Hippias, Kleisthenes, Miltiades, Kalliades and Peisistratos. The list was set up ca. 425 B.C., and was intended for the convenience of administration.

The inscription on the right (no. 3; I 2729) comes from the Library of Pantainos ㊽ (Fig. 74). On it are engraved library regulations dating from ca. 100 A.D.: "No book shall be removed since we have taken an oath to that effect. Open from the first hour till the sixth."

On the top shelf are two nonjoining fragments of a monument erected in memory of Athenians who fell fighting the Persians (I 303 = *IG* I³ 503–504b). The inscription consists of two epigrams, the first written on a smooth top margin, the second added on a specially dressed panel below. The general sense is certain. According to the first epigram the fallen, fighting both on land and sea, had saved Greece from slavery. The second epigram records the preservation of Athens from burning at the hands of the Persians. The latter poem in all probability refers to the Battle of Marathon (490 B.C.), but the relationship between the two epigrams is uncertain.

Tribute list: B. D. Meritt, *Hesperia* 8 (1939), pp. 54–59, no. 20; B. D. Meritt, H. T. Wade-Gery, and M. F. McGregor, *The Athenian Tribute Lists* 2 (1949), no. 33; *AgPicBk* 10 (1966), fig. 10; R. Meiggs and D. Lewis, *A Selection of Greek Historical Inscriptions* (1969), no. 75; L. Kallet, *Hesperia* 73 (2004), pp. 475–480. **Archon list**: B. D. Meritt, *Hesperia* 8 (1939), pp. 59–65, no. 21; D. Bradeen, *Hesperia* 32 (1963), pp. 187–205; *AgPicBk* 10 (1966), fig. 5; C. Pébarthe, *RÉA* 107 (2005), pp. 11–28. **Library rules**: T. L. Shear, *Hesperia* 5 (1936), pp. 41–42, fig. 40; *Agora* III (1957; reprinted 1973), no. 464; *AgPicBk* 10 (1966), fig. 32; *Agora* XIV (1972), p. 115. **Epigrams of the Persian Wars**: J. H. Oliver, *Hesperia* 2 (1933), pp. 480–494, no. 11; J. H. Oliver, *Hesperia* 5 (1936), pp. 225–234; B. D. Meritt, *AJP* 83 (1962), pp. 294–298; *AgPicBk* 10 (1966), fig. 2; R. Meiggs and D. Lewis, *A Selection of Greek Historical Inscriptions* (1969), no. 26; A. P. Matthaiou, *Horos* 14–16 (2000–2003), pp. 143–152.

CASES 29–30. *OSTRAKA*

Cases 29 and 30 display representative examples from the collection of some 1,500 *ostraka* found in the Agora (Fig. 75). These potsherds, called "ostraka" by the Greeks in both ancient and modern times, were used as ballots in the 5th century B.C. in the process of ostracism, which took its name from the ballots.

Figure 75. A selection of sherds (ostraka) *used in votes to exile prominent politicians in the 5th century B.C., naming Aristeides, Kimon, Themistokles, and Perikles (clockwise from left)*

At times when there was fear of a tyranny, a vote was held in the Agora. Each citizen wrote on his ballot the name of the man whom he feared. If as many as 6,000 ballots were cast, the proceeding was valid, and the man whose name appeared most frequently was exiled for a period of 10 years. Sherds of all sorts were used for the purpose: scraps of figured, black-gloss, and plain vases, roof tiles, well heads, etc. The writing, too, shows great variety even among ballots cast on the same day. The letters provide information about the (mis)spelling and pronunciation used by the average Athenian. For example, the name of the politician Themistokles is always spelled "Themisthokles," with a theta, not a tau, beginning the third syllable. The name of the man on the ballot is normally accompanied by that of his father or deme or both. Very occasionally the voter has given more precise expression to his feelings, as in the case of an *ostrakon* with the name of Xanthippos, father of Perikles (Case 30, no. 9; P 16873). It seems to speak to the reader:

> *This* ostrakon *says Xanthippos, son of Arriphron, does most wrong of the accursed leaders.* (trans. M. Lang)

Case 30 displays *ostraka* from the Agora proper on which appear the names of all the famous men known to have come up for ostracism from the earliest instance of its use (487 B.C.) to the latest (417 B.C.). Case 29 holds part of a hoard of 190 *ostraka* found in a well on the north slope of the Acropolis. All bear the name of Themistokles, and all are probably of the year 482 B.C. They must have been prepared in advance, presumably by some political club for the convenience of illiterate voters, but they seem not to have been used. Note the careful writing. Many pieces are by the same hand. While this cache may be taken as evidence for illiteracy, the variety of writing on the *ostraka* as a whole point to more people writing, rather than fewer.

Agora III (1957; reprinted 1973), pp. 163–165; *Agora* XIV (1972), pp. 50–51; E. Vanderpool in *Lectures in Memory of Louise Taft Semple* (Norman, Okla., 1973), pp. 215–270; *Agora* XXV (1990); *AgPicBk* 4 (revised 2004), pp. 20–21; J. P. Sickinger in *The Athenian Agora: New Perspectives on an Ancient Site* (Mainz, 2009), pp. 77–83.

OSTRACISM

Many of the activities associated with democracy took place in the Agora in permanent structures like the Tholos and Bouleuterion, but ostracism occurred only occasionally, so temporary spaces were arranged:

> *When it seemed good (to conduct an ostracism) the agora was fenced with boards, ten entrances being left, through which the citizens entered by tribes to place their sherds . . . the nine archons and the Council presided.*
> —Philoch., fr.. 30 (trans. R. E. Wycherley)

Because of the impermanence of the space, the primary physical remains are the *ostraka* themselves, the refuse swept up after the votes. These pieces provide information about the range of candidates, spelling and literacy, and the voting process. Many of them can be connected to historical figures, such as Perikles and Kimon. There are currently over 1,500 *ostraka* in the Agora collection, and almost 10,000 have been found in the Kerameikos nearby, most from a single cache of about 8,000.

The original intent of this procedure was to keep any one person from becoming too influential and raising himself up as a tyrant. The punishment was not dire. Unlike true exile, the "winner" of the vote had to leave for only 10 years, kept his property, and had a chance of being recalled if the people wanted him back. Xanthippos, father of Perikles, was said to be the first person not associated with the tyrants to be a victim of the vote. Despite the intent, people must have had a variety of reasons for their choices. Plutarch records an amusing anecdote about a citizen voting for a candidate whose honest behavior had earned him the nickname "The Just":

> *While the votes were being written down, an illiterate and uncouth rustic handed his piece of earthenware to Aristeides and asked him to write the*

name "Aristeides" on it. *The latter was astonished and asked the man what harm Aristeides had ever done him. "None whatever," was the reply. "I do not even know the fellow, but I am sick of hearing him called 'The Just' everywhere!" When he heard this, Aristeides said nothing, but wrote his name on the* ostrakon *and handed it back.*

—Plut., *Arist.* 7.5–6 (trans. I. Scott-Kilvert).

This very radical solution to power struggles was short-lived; the last recorded ostracism was held in 417 B.C. Plutarch tells us that it was abandoned because the process became a sham, used to aid the powerful rather than prevent their rise:

Now the sentence of ostracism was not a chastisement of base practices, nay, it was speciously called a humbling and docking of oppressive prestige and power; but it was really a merciful exorcism of the spirit of jealous hate, which thus vented its malignant desire to injure, not in some irreparable evil, but in a mere change of residence for ten years. And when ignoble men of the baser sort came to be subjected to this penalty, it ceased to be inflicted at all, and Hyperbolus was the last to be thus ostracized. It is said that Hyperbolus was ostracized for the following reason. Alcibiades and Nicias had the greatest power in the state, and were at odds. Accordingly, when the people were about to exercise the ostracism, and were clearly going to vote against one or the other of these two men, they came to terms with one another, united their opposing factions, and effected the ostracism of Hyperbolus. The people were incensed at this for they felt that the institution had been insulted and abused, and so they abandoned it utterly and put an end to it.

—Plut., *Arist.* 7.2–4 (trans. B. Perrin)

CASES 31–32. EQUIPMENT FOR THE LAW COURTS

A large group of Athenians were chosen yearly to serve as jurors, and from this group a jury was selected for each trial. The jury was made up of a minimum of 201 men, and larger assemblies of 1,000 or more are also known. Case 31 displays an allotment machine (*kleroterion*) used for randomized juror selection (I 3967). This clever device consisted of a marble *stele* in the front of which were one or more columns of slots of a size to receive the identity tickets of the jurors (Fig. 76). The number of columns varied according to the function of the machine; in this case there were 11. At the left edge are cuttings for the attachment of a vertical bronze tube. The allotment machines stood at the entrances to the law courts. The slots were filled with identity tickets. Bronze balls, some black and some white, were poured into the tube and released at the bottom one by one. Depending on whether a black or a white ball came out, the citizens represented by one entire row of name plates were either retained or rejected for jury service on that day. This machine, like all that have survived, is of the Hellenistic period. In the 4th century B.C. the machines were movable and presumably were made of wood. Note the drawing of a reconstruction of a typical machine on the wall.

In front of the *kleroterion* are samples of objects that were used with it. There are a number of the bronze identity tickets (*pinakia*, nos. 3–6) carried by all citizens eligible for jury service (Fig. 77). On each was incised the name of the bearer, his father, and his deme, and each bore an official stamp: an owl or a *gorgoneion*. The stamped letter indicates the bearer's jury section. Some of the *pinakia* retain traces of letters from an earlier use. These *pinakia* figure largely in Aristotle's account of court procedure, beginning with their use in the allotment machine. The small bronze ball shown with the identity tickets (no. 2) was also used in the allotment machine.

Also in this case are several wheel-shaped objects of bronze, some of which are inscribed "official ballot" (*psephos demosia*) (nos. 8–14). They correspond with Aristotle's account (*Ath. Pol.* 68) of the ballots used by the Athenian jurors for recording their votes. The ballots with solid axles were for acquittal, the hollow for condemnation (Fig. 78). The six solid ballots displayed here were found together in the ruins of a building of the 5th and 4th centuries B.C. beneath the north end of the Stoa of Attalos ➍. They are good evidence for

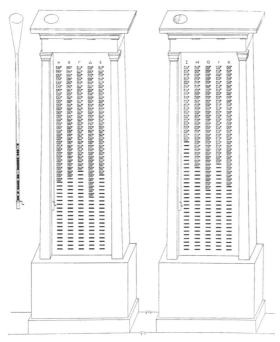

Figure 76. Allotment machine (kleroterion) *used to pick jurors for a trial,* *photograph and restored drawing*

Figure 77 (top). Official juror's identification tag, 4th century B.C. The inscription reads: "Demophanes the son of Phil[- - -], of the township of Kephisia."

Figure 78 (bottom). Inscribed jurors' ballots, 4th century B.C.

identifying the building as a law court. A plan of this building and a photo of the ballot box can be seen on the sides of the case.

The unglossed lid of a cooking pot or *echinos* (no. 7; P 28470) carries a painted inscription which, though fragmentary, seems to list documents stored and sealed in the pot until their presentation at a trial (Fig. 79). It dates to the 4th century B.C., and was found in the northeast area of the Agora.

Case 32 displays a unique example of a waterclock (*klepsydra*) used for measuring speeches in the law courts (P 2084). It was regarded

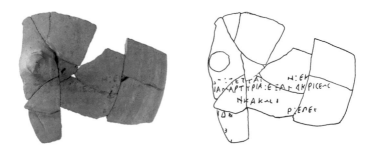

Figure 79. Lid of a small pot used to hold evidence until the time of a trial, 4th century B.C. (photo and drawing). The inscription probably reads: "Of the written copies, the following four are inside: diamartyria *(testimony) from the* anakrisis *(arbitration), law on the abuse of heiresses, challenge of testimony, oaths of litigants. Antenor put the lid on." (trans. A. Boegehold)*

Figure 80. Terracotta waterclock in use (original in foreground, plaster replica in background)

by the ancients themselves as the most characteristic feature of the courts. Shaped like a modern flower pot, but with two handles, the vessel has a small, bronze-lined outlet at the bottom, and a larger hole under the rim to allow the vessel to be filled to exactly the same level each time (Fig. 80). The lower hole was closed with a stopper until the speaker began; the plug was then withdrawn and the speaker might continue as long as the water ran, in this case 6 minutes. The capacity is indicated by the painted inscription "XX" on the wall of the vessel, i.e., two *choes* (6.4 liters or 1.7 gallons). The inscription is more visible on the copy in the background. Also on the wall are faint traces of the word "Antiochis," the name of one of the 10 tribes of Athens. The waterclock was found in a well of the late 5th century B.C. at the southwest corner of the Agora **8**.

Equipment for trials: *Agora* XIV (1972), pp. 52–56; *Hesperia* Suppl. 19 (1982), pp. 1–6; J. McK. Camp II, *The Athenian Agora* (London, 1986), pp. 107–113; *Agora* XXVIII (1995); *AgPicBk* 23 (1994), figs. 13, 28, 29, 36; *AgPicBk* 4 (revised 2004), pp. 22–26; J. McK. Camp II in *The Athenian Agora: New Perspectives on an Ancient Site* (Mainz, 2009), pp. 20–22. ***Kleroteria***: *Hesperia* Suppl. 1 (1937), pp. 198–215 (I 3967 = no. X); S. Dow, *HSCP* 50 (1939), pp. 1–34. ***Klepsydra***: A. Paterakis, *OSGP* 5 (1997), p. 80; J. K. Papadopoulos et al. in *The Art of Antiquity* (Athens, 2007), p. 172.

CASE 4. SOKRATES IN THE AGORA

Before continuing with some of the public material along the left side of the gallery, return to the central case.

The back of the case holds material from buildings associated with the life and death of Sokrates. The hollow bone eyelets for laces and the iron hobnails used for shoemaking (Fig. 81; nos. 4 and 5) come from a 5th century house ❾ which lay just outside the Agora adjacent to the boundary stone near the Tholos. The fragment of a black-gloss drinking cup (no. 6) was found nearby and presumably identifies the owner of the cobbler's shop as Simon. Xenophon, Diogenes Laertius, and Plutarch tell us that Sokrates, when he wished to meet those students too young to enter the Agora, would see them at the house of Simon the cobbler, which stood nearby. The rest of the material in the case comes from a building southwest of the main square, tentatively identified as the State Prison ⓻, where Sokrates was put to death. Thirteen small medicine bottles (Fig. 82; no. 2) found in a cistern in the building represent a remarkable concentration of this rare shape, and a small marble statuette (Fig. 83; S 1413), perhaps of Sokrates himself, was found in the building as well. Also in this case (on long-term loan) is a red-figure cup featuring athletes at an exercise court (*palaestra*). Its findspot was also the prison (Fig. 84; P 30987).

General: *AgPicBk* 17 (1978). **House of Simon**: D. B. Thompson, *Archaeology* 13 (1960), pp. 234–240; *Agora* XIV (1972), pp. 173–174. **Cup with inscription**: *Agora* XXI (1976), p. 36, no. F 86. **Prison(?)**: M. Crosby, *Hesperia* 20 (1951), pp. 168–187; *Agora* III (1957; reprinted 1973), pp. 149–150; E. Vanderpool, *From Athens to Gordion* (Philadelphia, 1980), pp. 17–31; V. Hunter, *Phoenix* 51 (1997), pp. 296–326; S. I. Rotroff in *The Athenian Agora: New Perspectives on an Ancient Site* (Mainz, 2009), pp. 44–45. **Medicine bottles**: *Agora* XXIX (1997), p. 370, no. 1309.

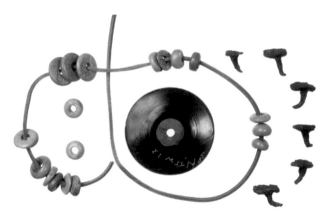

Figure 81 (top). Bone eyelets, iron hobnails, and the base of a black-gloss drinking cup inscribed with the name Simon

Figure 82 (middle). Set of 13 clay medicine bottles, 4th century B.C.

Figure 83 (bottom). Fragmentary marble statuette, possibly of Sokrates, 4th century B.C.

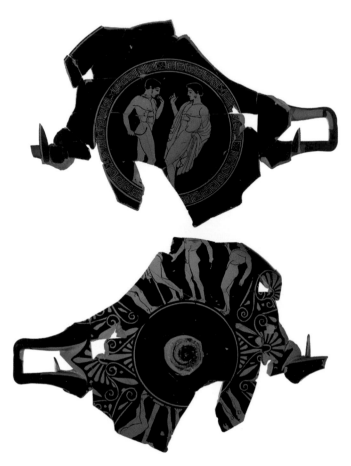

Figure 84. Red-figure cup with palaestra *scene, tondo and exterior, late 5th century* B.C.

CASE 4. BRONZE HEAD OF NIKE (VICTORY)

The head, about half life size, comes from a winged Nike (Fig. 85; B 30). The V-shaped termination below was designed to fit into a socket in the bust. The topknot, drawn up and tied ponytail-style, has been lost; it was cast separately and attached to the peg at the crown of the head. The eyes, also missing, were made in separate capsules and inset. Channels encircle the head just below the hair; they also run up to the top of the skull from front and back and down the neck on either side. Traces of earlier channels, now packed with bronze, may be detected on the back of the neck and on the sides of the skull. In

Figure 85. Bronze head of Nike, ca. 420–415 B.C.: (left) photograph; (right) watercolor restoring the head with hair.

the channel above the forehead is a piece of sheet silver. Behind the ears are small masses of gold above silver. It appears that the head (as also the torso) was once covered with sheets of silver and above the silver with gold fastened in such a way that the precious metal could be removed. For this reason, the figure has been identified as one of the "Golden Nikai" which are known from the ancient authors and inscriptions to have served as repositories for the state's gold reserve in the 5th and 4th centuries B.C. These were twice stripped of their precious metal to help meet financial crises, first toward the end of the 5th century and again at the beginning of the 3rd. That this statue, made ca. 420–415 B.C., is too small to hold the two talents of gold required of each Nike suggests another purpose for it, however. It was found in a well of the late 3rd century B.C. at the west side of the Agora. Another gilded bronze may be seen in Case 65 (pp. 155–156, the bronze equestrian statue).

T. L. Shear, *Hesperia* 2 (1933), pp. 519–527; H. A. Thompson, *HSCP* Suppl. 1 (1940), pp. 183–210; D. B. Thompson, *Hesperia* 13 (1944), pp. 173–209; *Agora* XIV (1972), pp. 190–191; C. C. Mattusch, *Classical Bronzes* (Ithaca, 1996), pp. 30–31, 121–125, 128–129.

CASE 68. OFFICIAL WEIGHTS AND MEASURES; CLAY AND LEAD TOKENS

A set of official weights and measures was kept in the Tholos ❺. The law required that weights and measures to be used in commerce should first be checked against these standards. The excavations around the Tholos have brought to light official examples dating from the 6th, 5th, and 4th centuries B.C., and a few others have been found elsewhere in the area. These provide evidence for the absolute values of the ancient units. Numerous commercial weights and one measure have been found in the ruins of houses and shops. They show greater deviations from the standard than would be tolerated today.

On the bottom shelf, center, is a set of three bronze weights (nos. 21–23) of ca. 500 B.C. found in a well near the Tholos. All are inscribed "official property of the people of Athens." On each weight the denomination is indicated both in writing and by a symbol:

> stater = knucklebone (810 grams)
> quarter (stater) = shield (199.5 grams)
> sixth (stater) = tortoise (127.5 grams)

The lead commercial weights shown with them (nos. 24–30) are also marked both in writing and with symbols:

> two staters = wheel (1,792.5 grams)
> stater = knucklebone (841.5 grams)
> mina = dolphin (455 grams)
> third (stater) = *amphora* (301 grams)
> quarter (stater) = tortoise (231 grams)
> sixth (stater) = half *amphora* (156.5 grams)
> eighth (stater) = half tortoise (105 grams)

On the top shelf of the case is a tall cylindrical measure of terracotta found in a well on the north slope of the Acropolis (no. 1; AP 1103); it dates to the third quarter of the 5th century B.C. The Y-shaped bar in the mouth was intended to facilitate leveling, indicating that the vessel was a dry measure. Its official character is indicated by the inscription painted around the middle: "official" (*demosion*), and by the owl stamped on the wall just below the lip. The capacity is 3.2 liters (0.85 gallons), i.e., 3 ancient *choinikes*.

Figure 86. *An assortment of official dry measures for grain and nuts, 5th–2nd centuries* B.C., *with detail of Athena stamp at right*

To the right (no. 2) is another cylindrical dry measure, likewise inscribed "official" (*demosion*) and stamped on the wall with the head of Athena and a double-bodied owl (Fig. 86; P 3559). Dating from the 4th century B.C., it was found near the Tholos ❺. Its capacity is about 1.7 liters (0.45 gallons), the equivalent of 1½ *choinikes*. For an official measure in bronze, see Case 38 (p. 165).

At the end (no. 3) is a third dry measure, more coarsely made and with its wall bent out to form a wide rim (Fig. 86; P 14431). It comes from the ruins of a house and dates to ca. 100 B.C. On the outer end of a mass of lead set through the wall is stamped a figure of the seated Dionysos. The capacity is about 1.7 liters (0.45 gallons), i.e., 1½ *choinikes*. The vessel conforms to the specifications in an Athenian law of the late 2nd century B.C. for the measure to be used in the sale of various fruits and nuts. The lead seal was applied by the officials in the Tholos after checking against a standard measure.

On the shelf below (no. 1) is a small pitcher (*olpe*) of ca. 500 B.C. with the painted delta-epsilon ligature $\cancel{E}$ for *demosion* (P 13429). This will have been a standard liquid measure; it holds 0.252 liters, the capacity of the ancient *kotyle* (1/12th of a *chous*). Beside the *olpe* is a small black drinking cup (*kylix*) of the second quarter of the 5th century B.C. (no. 2; P 5117). Scratched on its floor is the same ligature meaning "official." The cup, found in a well below the Stoa of Zeus ㉕, might have been used in some nearby public dining hall. The marble washbasin of which a fragment is shown next to the cup also served a public body (no. 3; I 4869). According to the inscription on its rim it belonged to the Bouleuterion (Council House). It was found just south of the Old Bouleuterion ⑭ and can be dated from its letter forms to the early 5th century B.C.

The three little terracotta plaques on the far right of this shelf (nos. 31–33), each with one end cut in a jagged line, are *symbola*, i.e., "things to be fitted together" (MC 820–822). They were made in the shape of dominoes and inscribed on both faces. On one side, above, was written the name of a deme; below appears the abbreviation for an office, pol[–], probably for *poletes,* an official auctioneer. On the other side across the middle was written the name of a tribe. Before baking, the plaque was cut through the middle in a jagged line. After baking, the parts were presumably distributed and subsequently reunited, possibly in connection with allotment to a deme office, or to establish the identity of a messenger. The tablets were found in a deposit of the third quarter of the 5th century B.C. behind the Stoa of Attalos ㊻.

The rest of the material on the bottom self is associated with the Athenian army and cavalry. No. 19 (B 1373) is a spear butt,

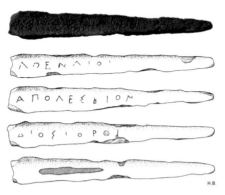

which would have been attached to the end of the wooden shaft of a spear to counterbalance the heavy metal point (Fig. 87). It carries the incised inscription: "The Athenians from the Lesbians (dedicated this) to the Dioskouroi." It should date to 428/7 B.C., therefore, when the Athenians suppressed a revolt of their allies on the island of Lesbos (Thuc. 3).

Figure 87. Bronze spear-butt taken from the Lesbians in 428/7 B.C., dedicated to the Dioskouroi (photograph and drawing)

The lead tablet (no. 20) and round stamped clay tokens (nos. 11–18) are part of a cavalry archive found in a well by the crossroads at the northwest corner of the Agora ㉗ (see the *Agora Site Guide*, p. 86). The lead strips, which were found rolled up, carry the name of a man and the color, brand, and value of his horse (Fig. 88). Horses of the Athenian cavalry were apparently inspected and registered on a regular basis. The clay tokens are stamped with the name of an official:

Figure 88. Lead tablet describing a horse from the Athenian cavalry: "Belonging to Konon, a chestnut with a centaur brand, worth 700 drachma" (photograph and drawing).

"Pheidon, the hipparch (cavalry commander) in Lemnos" (Fig. 89). The same officer is known as a trainer of young cavalrymen in a fragment of the comic poet Mnesimachos (Ath. 9.402):

> Go forth, Manes, to the Agora, to the Herms, the place
> frequented by the phylarchs, and to their handsome pupils,
> whom Pheidon trains in mounting and dismounting.

Figure 89. Clay tokens stamped with the name of Pheidon, the hipparch in Lemnos, who was responsible for training cavalry recruits in the Agora, 4th century B.C.

Figure 90. Lead tokens used for the issuing of pieces of armor: greaves, breast-plates, helmet, and shield.

Presumably the tokens were used in a messenger system or as passports of some sort. The two rectangular clay tokens (nos. 34 and 35; SS 8080, MC 1245) are similarly official, used by Xenokles the peripolarch (border commander).

The small round lead tokens behind the weights (nos. 4–10) were also used by the army, apparently for the issuing of armor (Fig. 90). Each disk is stamped on one side with a letter of the alphabet, while the other side has a representation of a piece of armor: helmet, breast-plate, greaves, and shields are all represented.

Weights and measures: *Agora* X (1964); *AgPicBk* 4 (revised 2004), pp. 30–32; J. McK. Camp II in *The Athenian Agora: New Perspectives on an Ancient Site* (Mainz, 2009), pp. 19–20, 22–23. **P 5117**: *Agora* XII (1970), p. 265, no. 436; *Agora* XXI (1976), no. Fa 2. **Symbola**: H. A. Thompson, *Hesperia* 20 (1951), pp. 51–52; *AgPicBk* 4 (revised 2004), pp. 15–16. **Military objects**: J. H. Kroll, *Hesperia* 46 (1977), pp. 83–140 (lead cavalry tablets); J. H. Kroll, *Hesperia* 46 (1977), pp. 141–146 (lead tokens); J. H. Kroll and F. W. Mitchel, *Hesperia* 49 (1980), pp. 86–96 (clay tokens); G. R. Bugh, *The Horsemen of Athens* (Princeton, 1988); *AgPicBk* 24 (1998), pp. 31–38; *AgPicBk* 4 (revised 2004), pp. 10–12; J. McK. Camp II in *The Athenian Agora: New Perspectives on an Ancient Site* (Mainz, 2009), pp. 27–29. **Spear butt**: J. McK. Camp II, *Hesperia* 47 (1978), pp. 192–195; J. McK. Camp II in *The Athenian Agora: New Perspectives on an Ancient Site* (Mainz, 2009), pp. 35–37.

(FREESTANDING) DECREE AGAINST TYRANNY

Next to Case 68 stands a complete marble *stele* inscribed with a law passed by the people of Athens in 336 B.C. (Fig. 91; I 6524). The law, proposed by Eukrates, son of Aristotimos of Peiraeus, was intended to discourage attempts to set up a tyranny, i.e., a dictatorship:

> *If anyone rise up against the people with a view to tyranny,*
> *or join in establishing tyranny, or overthrow the People of*
> *the Athenians or the Democracy in Athens, whoever kills*
> *him who does any of these things shall be blameless.*

If, however, a tyranny were to be established, the law prohibited the Council of the Areopagus, which was still looked upon as the guardian of the constitution, from meeting. In this way a tyrant who had achieved power *de facto* was prevented from gaining *de jure* recognition. Two copies of the law were to be engraved on marble *stelai* and set up, one near the entrance to the meeting place of the Council of the Areopagus, the other in the meeting place of the Assembly. A sum of 20 drachmas was appropriated for the making of the *stelai*. The text is illustrated by a relief in which Democracy places a wreath on the head of the People of Athens.

The law was passed a few months after Philip II of Macedon had broken the power of Thebes and of Athens at Chaironeia (338 B.C.). It was directed against the possibility of a pro-Macedonian revolt in Athens. The effective life of the law, however, was short. In 322 B.C. the Macedonians occupied Athens. Eukrates, the proposer of the law, is reported to have perished miserably. The marble copies of his law were presumably pulled down; the surviving *stele* was discovered in the building fill of the Square Peristyle that was under construction in the late 4th century at the northeast corner of the Agora ❹ (see also the *Agora Site Guide,* pp. 104–105).

B. D. Meritt, *Hesperia* 21 (1952), pp. 355–389, no. 5; M. Ostwald, *TAPA* 86 (1955), pp. 103–128; J. Pouilloux, *Choix d'inscriptions grecques* (Paris, 1960), no. 32; C. L. Lawton, *Attic Document Reliefs* (Oxford, 1995), pp. 99–100, no. 38; P. J. Rhodes and R. Osborne, *Greek Historical Inscriptions* (Oxford, 2003), no. 79; *AgPicBk* 4 (revised 2004), pp. 18–19.

Figure 91. Decree against tyranny, 336 B.C., with a relief showing the People (Demos) *being crowned by Democracy*

CASE 67. SPARTAN SHIELD FROM THE BATTLE OF PYLOS

The shield (B 262) is of the type normally carried by a heavy-armed warrior (hoplite) in the 5th century B.C. (Fig. 92). Its border is adorned with a rich braid pattern. The metal has the thickness of heavy paper and may have been lined with leather or some other material.

Punched through the bronze in large letters is the inscription, "The Athenians from the Lakedaemonians from Pylos." Since the letter forms are of the late 5th century B.C., the shield may be identified as one of those carried by the 292 Spartans captured by the Athenians at Pylos in 425 B.C. (Thuc. 4.8). The spectacle of Spartans surrendering alive made a great impression on the Greek world. The Athenians proudly hung the Spartan shields in the Painted Stoa ㉟ where some were still seen by Pausanias in the 2nd century A.D. The museum's example was removed earlier for some reason; it was later used as the lid of a cistern to the south of the Hephaisteion ❶ and was buried when the cistern was abandoned in the 3rd century B.C.

T. L. Shear, *Hesperia* 6 (1937), pp. 346–348; T. L. Shear, *ArchEph* 1937 A′, pp. 140–143; *Agora* XIV (1972), pp. 92–93; *AgPicBk* 4 (revised 2004), pp. 12–13; J. McK. Camp II in *The Athenian Agora: New Perspectives on an Ancient Site* (Mainz, 2009), pp. 35–36.

Figure 92. Bronze shield taken by the Athenians from the Spartans at Pylos, 425 B.C., and displayed as a trophy in the Painted Stoa: photograph (left); drawing showing punched inscription and guilloche pattern (right).

CASE 66. HEADS OF MARBLE HERMS

Because Athens was noted for the number of Herms—representations of the god Hermes in the form of a four-sided post with an anthropomorphized head and phallus—that stood in both public and private places, it is not surprising that many were recovered in the excavation of the Agora. Three heads of various types are exhibited here (Fig. 93; see the *Agora Site Guide*, pp. 82–83).

No. 1 (S 3347) is from a life-size Herm of white marble, with corkscrew curls over the forehead, full beard, and moustache. Though somewhat battered, the almond-shaped eyes and upward-curving, deep-set mouth allow this head to be dated to ca. 510–500 B.C., making this one of the earlier Herms found in Athens. It was found in Byzantine fill on the west foundations of the Painted Stoa **35**.

The slightly smaller than life-size head of Parian marble (no. 2; S 2452) is a casualty of the scandalous mutilation of the Herms in 415 B.C. It was excavated among the votives of the late 5th century B.C. in the Crossroads Enclosure **27**. The head has a full beard and moustache. A broad, flat headband rises to a peak in front and is tied behind with cords. The band divides the hair into two parts: the front hair is swept back in a naturalistic way into voluminous masses above the ears; behind the band the hair is combed in fine regular ridges that radiate from the crown and descend down the back under the band

Figure 93. Three Herm heads found at the northwest corner of the Agora (from left to right): 2nd century A.D., late 5th century B.C., and early 5th century B.C.

to end in a slight flourish at shoulder height. The lower lip is inset, presumably because of some mishap in the carving. The style of the head, combined with its fresh condition, indicates that it had been made only a few years before its destruction.

The slightly smaller than life-size head of Pentelic marble (no. 3; S 2499) dates to the 2nd century A.D., and was found in a context of the 4th century A.D. in the two-aisled stoa ㉙ just to the west of the Royal Stoa. In type, this head belongs to a large group of replicas that are connected by two inscribed examples with the Athenian sculptor Alkamenes (active ca. 430–410 B.C.). Characteristic are the three rows of corkscrew curls arched over the forehead and the finely combed hair radiating from the crown, falling in a heavy mass down the back with a single ringlet brought forward from behind the ear to descend over the shoulder. A twisted band encircles the head. The beard and moustache are luxuriant, the lips full.

S 3347: T. L. Shear Jr., *Hesperia* 53 (1984), pp. 42–43. S 2452: T. L. Shear Jr., *Hesperia* 42 (1973), pp. 164–165. S 2499: T. L. Shear Jr., *Hesperia* 42 (1973), pp. 406–407.

CASE 65. FRAGMENTS FROM A GILDED BRONZE EQUESTRIAN STATUE

The bronze leg, sword, and drapery fragment (B 1382–1384) came from a large gilded bronze statue of a figure on horseback, probably of Demetrios Poliorketes, Macedonian ruler of Athens late in the 4th century B.C. (Fig. 94). The pieces were found discarded in the public well near the northwest crossroads ㉗ (see the *Agora Site Guide,* p. 86) in a level dating to ca. 200 B.C., a time of strong anti-Macedonian feeling. The leg is hollow cast, the sword solid bronze. Note the traces of gilding.

The image on the wall of the reconstructed gate with statue provides only an idea of how it might have been displayed; there is no firm evidence that this is where this statue stood.

Figure 94. Bronze leg with drapery, and sword from a gilded bronze equestrian statue, late 4th century B.C.

T. L. Shear Jr., *Hesperia* 42 (1973), pp. 165–168; J. McK. Camp II, *The Athenian Agora* (London, 1986), pp. 162–165; C. C. Mattusch, *Classical Bronzes* (Ithaca, 1996), pp. 125–129; *AgPicBk* 24 (1998), pp. 20–21.

🡒 Cross to the right side of the gallery to begin the exploration of pottery. Cases 33–36 are devoted to Athenian painted pottery of the Archaic and Classical Periods.

CASE 33–34. ARCHAIC BLACK-FIGURE POTTERY

In Case 33, the three drinking cups (*skyphoi*) of generous proportions (top shelf, nos. 1 and 2; bottom shelf, no. 4) are all works of the Theseus Painter of ca. 500 B.C. Note especially no. 1 (photo p. 10, bottom center; P 1546) on which boys riding piggyback engage in the game called *ephedrismos,* the same activity that has been suggested for the sculpture from the Hephaisteion (S 429, pp. 45–46).

The numerous oil flasks (*lekythoi*) in Case 34 are decorated with a variety of scenes. One large example (Fig. 95; P 24104, on long-term loan) bears an unusual version of a commonly illustrated theme of the introduction of Herakles into Olympos.

On the top shelf (no. 6; P 12628) is a perfume bottle (*alabastron*) decorated by the Amasis Painter with a frieze of quietly standing divinities. This is a good example of the miniature painting that was popular in the middle of the 6th century B.C. The full scene can be enjoyed in the watercolor on the wall behind it.

In the center of the bottom shelf is a good example of the "Siana" type of drinking cup (no. 3; P 20716: ca. 570 B.C.). On the floor medallion (tondo) is a running warrior; on the exterior on either side is a grazing horse. The fragment of a Panathenaic *amphora* (lower right, no. 9; P 1893) is one of many such found in the Agora. The practice of giving jars of olive oil to victorious athletes at the Panathenaic Festival persisted through the Hellenistic and Roman periods, as is attested by this piece, which dates to the late 4th century B.C.

General pottery: *Agora* XII (1970); *Agora* XXIII (1986); *Agora* XXX (1997); K. M. Lynch in *The Art of Antiquity* (Athens, 2007), pp. 178–220. **Theseus Painter** *skyphoi*: E. Vanderpool, *Hesperia* 15 (1946), pp. 289–291; J. D. Beazley, *Attic Black-Figure Vase-Painters* (Oxford, 1956), p. 518, nos. 4, 47, 54; *Agora* XXIII (1986), pp. 279–280, nos. 1484, 1486, 1490. **Amasis** *alabastron*: E. Vanderpool, *Hesperia* 8 (1939), pp. 247–266; J. D. Beazley, *Paralipomena* (Oxford, 1971), p. 64, no. 64; *Agora* XXIII (1986),

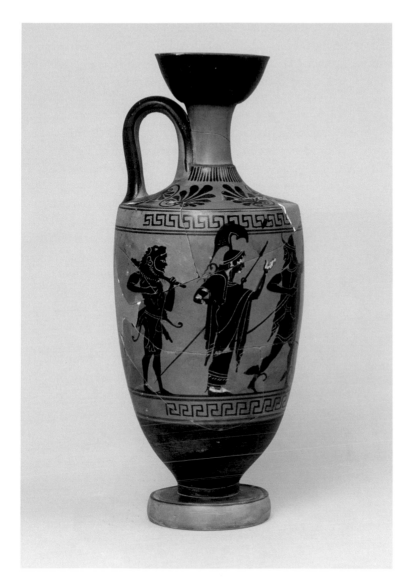

Figure 95. Black-figure lekythos *depicting the introduction of Herakles into Olympos, ca. 510–500 B.C.*

p. 253, no. 1257. **Siana cup**: E. Vanderpool, *Hesperia* 20 (1951), pp. 61–63; J. D. Beazley, *Paralipomena* (Oxford, 1971), p. 25; *Agora* XXIII (1986), pp. 299–300, no. 1678.
Panathenaic *amphora* fragment: G. R. Edwards, *Hesperia* 26 (1957), p. 342, no. 23.

CASE 35. ARCHAIC RED-FIGURE POTTERY

This case is devoted to red-figure drinking cups (often referred to as *kylikes*). In addition to style and scene-types, many of these pieces also tell us about context and workshops: some were found together, and others were painted by the same hand.

The red-figure cups on the top shelf all date to the late 6th century. The one to the left (Fig. 96; no. 1; P 24113) nicely illustrates the range of subject matter popular with Athenian vase painters of the time. The floor medallion (tondo) depicts a youth bearing a hare, presumably as a love gift. On the exterior, side A shows the duel between Achil-

les and Memnon in the presence of their mothers. Side B depicts a Dionysiac revel. In the field of the medallion is the signature of the potter, "Gorgos made me." On the outside of the cup is the love-name "Krates." Greek vases of this period often featured such erotically charged exclamations of a youth's beauty (e.g., "Krates *kalos*," or "Krates is beautiful").

Figure 96. Red-figure cup, late 6th century B.C.: (top) youth with hare in tondo; (bottom) Achilles fighting Memnon on the exterior.

The other two cups on the shelf are by the same Athenian painter, Epiktetos. The one in the center has a satyr on a donkey in the medallion (no. 2; P 24114). Only the medallion of the other is painted: a naked girl hurries away from a foot-bath carrying her shoes in her hands (no. 3; P 24131). In the field is the love-name "Hipparchos." This cup was found in the same well beneath the Stoa of Attalos **44** as the cup made by Gorgos (no. 1).

On the bottom shelf, the three large cups at the back of the case (nos. 1–3) are all by the Chairias Painter and were found together in the same well beneath the south end of the Stoa of Attalos **44** as nos. 1 and 3 on the top shelf: the subjects are a nude woman at an altar (P 24102), a maenad (P 24116), and a lyre player (P 24115). In front of them (no. 5; P 23165) is a fourth cup by the same painter, a fragment showing a woman washing. It was found in a different well near the southwest corner of the Agora. The date of all of these is ca. 500 B.C.

The three smaller cups resting on their feet in the front of the case (nos. 6–8; P 1272–P 1274) are attributed to unnamed painters referred to as the Group of Acropolis 96. They and the larger cup at the back corner of the case (no. 4; P 1275) were all found to the northeast of the Hephaisteion **1** in a deep shaft which had been used as a dumping place by neighboring potters. All four cups have single figures in their floor medallions: an athlete with jumping weights (P 1272), a castanet player (P 1273), a man playing *kottabos,* a game that involved throwing wine at a target from a drinking cup (Fig. 101; P 1274), and a boy hurrying along with two wine jars on a shoulder pole (P 1275). They date to ca. 500 B.C.

One final cup (Fig. 97; P 2698, on long-term loan) is of technical interest, a good example of the intentional combination of red figure with coral-red gloss, a fashion popular in Athens especially in the late 6th and early 5th centuries B.C.

General pottery: *Agora* XII (1970); *Agora* XXIII (1986); *Agora* XXX (1997); K. M. Lynch in *The Art of Antiquity* (Athens, 2007), pp. 178–220. **Cups from Stoa well**: L. Talcott and B. Philippaki in H. A. Thompson, *Hesperia* 24 (1955), pp. 63–66; J. D. Beazley, *Paralipomena* (Oxford, 1971), p. 334, no. 242 (P 24113); p. 328, no. 80 (P 24131; number incorrectly cited as 24138); *Agora* XXX (1997), pp. 317–318, 339, nos. 1407, 1554. **Chairias Painter**: L. Talcott, *Hesperia* 24 (1955), pp. 72–75; *Agora* XXX (1997), pp. 335, 341–343, 345, nos. 1520, 1562, 1574, 1594. **Cups from Rock-Cut Shaft**: J. D. Beazley, *Attic Red-Figure Vase-Painters* (Oxford, 1942), p. 67,

Figure 97. Cup with coral-red gloss technique, ca. 500 B.C.

nos. V 1–4; E. Vanderpool, *Hesperia* 15 (1946), pp. 279–280, nos. 33–36; *Agora* XXX (1997), pp. 340, 342, nos. 1555, 1571–1573. **Coral-red cup**: E. Vanderpool, *Hesperia* 15 (1946), pp. 285–287, no 52; *Agora* XXX (1997), p. 341, no. 1566.

CASE 36. CLASSICAL RED-FIGURE AND WHITE-GROUND POTTERY

Case 36 contains selections from a deposit of slender red-figure pitchers (*oinochoai*) found on the north slope of the Acropolis (top shelf, nos. 1 and 2; bottom shelf, no. 2). The shape is unusual, and the painted scenes still more so. On the body of P 15845 (top shelf, no. 2) is a four-horse chariot with a groom at the horses' heads. Athena was possibly at the reins. In two instances Athena appears on the neck of the vase, as Promachos, "first in battle" (one is P 14793, top shelf, no. 1). The goddess is rendered in an archaistic style comparable with that of the Panathenaic amphoras. On the front of the vase a pair of breasts stands out in high relief (P 15845; restored on P 15840, bottom shelf). The style of painting dates the vessels to the closing years of the 5th century B.C. The prominence of Athena and the place where the oinochoes were found suggest some sacred or civic use, perhaps in connection with the Panathenaic Festival.

The white-ground pieces on the top shelf are both of high quality. In the medallion of the white-ground cup (no. 5; P 43: ca. 480–470 B.C.) a youth tunes his lyre while his pet hare listens attentively. In the field is the love-name "Erinos." On a fragmentary bobbin next to it (no. 4; P 5113), Helios the sun god rises with his winged horses above the whitecrested waves (Fig. 98).

Figure 98. White-ground bobbin with depiction of Helios, ca. 480 B.C.

The red-figure wine jug (*chous*) at the right on the bottom shelf (photo p. 10, bottom right; no. 5; P 15210) can probably be connected with the spring festival called the *Anthesteria.* The spirit of revelry has invaded even a bronze foundry: a slave bearing an offering tray approaches the head of the establishment, who stands in holiday attire in front of his smelting furnace.

General pottery: *Agora* XII (1970); *Agora* XXIII (1986); *Agora* XXX (1997); K. M. Lynch in *The Art of Antiquity* (Athens, 2007), pp. 178–220. **North slope** *oinochoai*: R. Green, *Hesperia* 31 (1962), pp. 82–94; *Agora* XXX (1997), pp. 254, 256, nos. 809, 812, 823. **White-ground cup**: L Talcott, *Hesperia* 2 (1933), pp. 224–230; J. D. Beazley, *Attic Red-Figure Vase-Painters* (Oxford, 1942), p. 923; *Agora* XXX (1997), p. 342, no. 1570. **White-ground bobbin**: L. Talcott, *Hesperia* 5 (1936), pp. 333–335; *Agora* XXX (1997), p. 351, no. 1640. *Chous*: G. van Hoorn, *Choes and Anthesteria* (Leiden, 1951), p. 90, no. 227; *Agora* XXX (1997), p. 244, no. 716.

CASE 37. BLACK-FIGURE CALYX *KRATER* BY EXEKIAS(?)

Standing alone in its own case is a mixing bowl (*krater*) found in a well high on the north slope of the Acropolis (Fig. 99; AP 1044). It had perhaps been dedicated on the Acropolis and subsequently discarded. The *krater* was mended in antiquity, which demonstrates that it was esteemed by its owners. The vase is the earliest known example of the calyx *krater* shape. On one side (facing the right side of the case), the battle rages over the body of the fallen Patroklos; the other side preserves the front part of the procession that accompanied Herakles

Figure 99. Black-figure krater, mid-6th century B.C.: (left) battle over Patroklos; (right) procession of Herakles to Olympos.

to his deification on Olympos. In a lower zone on either side is a little picture of lions taking down a bull, likely inspired by pedimental compositions. On the handle side is an oblique allusion to the festive purpose of the vessel: above the handle a maenad sits in the shade of a grapevine, unaware as yet of the long-tailed satyr who hurries up from below.

Originally attributed to Exekias, the leading black-figure painter of the middle of the 6th century B.C., it now seems likely that the *krater* was painted instead by a contemporary artist, also highly skilled.

General pottery: *Agora* XII (1970); *Agora* XXIII (1986); *Agora* XXX (1997); K. M. Lynch in *The Art of Antiquity* (Athens, 2007), pp. 178–220. **Krater**: O. Broneer, *Hesperia* 6 (1937), pp. 468–486; O. Broneer, *AJA* 42 (1938), p. 445; J. D. Beazley, *Attic Black-Figure Vase-Painters* (Oxford, 1956), pp. 145–146, no. 19; E. A. Mackay, *Tradition and Originality* (Oxford, 2010), pp. 354–357.

LIFE AT HOME

The material found in the wells associated with homes just outside the Agora square provide insight into the private lives of Athenians, especially women, who were typically kept out of the more public sphere of politics, courts, and the military.

The Greek word for home was *oikos,* the root of the English word "economy." This etymology is telling: the Greek house was an economic center, not just a place to sleep and eat. The ivory seal buried with a wealthy woman in the Geometric period has been connected to her authority over household goods (Case 16, p. 116), and a broken plate inscribed with a kitchen inventory might be another artifact of household administration (Case 41, p. 168). Clothing manufacture—the spinning of wool into yarn and the weaving of that yarn into garments—was an important female skill, and the many spindle whorls and loomweights on display attest to that occupation. Food production was made easier by portable cooking implements such as grills and braziers (Cases 60–64, 40–42, pp. 167–168). Women collected water for household use from either wells in their own courtyards or from one of the public fountains, such as those at the southeast 62 and southwest corners 70 of the Agora square. Childcare—raising the next generation of Athenians—was another important household activity. The child's chair (Fig. 100) in Case 26 (pp. 126–127) controlled

Figure 100. Child using the potty chair

Figure 101. Man playing the drinking-game kottabos *on a red-figure cup, ca. 510 B.C.*

a toddler's movement when other matters required attention and promoted potty training too.

Although the house was arguably the sphere of women, men held sway over one section of it, the so-called *andron*. This room was usually the most decorative because it was the only one seen by outside guests when they attended a symposium, a communal drinking party. Here men reclined while sharing food and drink, discussed politics or philosophy, and made important social connections (Fig. 101). It was believed that one could tell a lot about a man's character by the way he behaved at these semiprivate events. The symposium was a microcosm of the city-state itself.

Much of the finer pottery in the Athenian home was intended for entertaining at the symposium. The event required specific drinking accoutrements, from pouring vessels like the *oinochoe* to cups for the individual drinkers. The most important vessel was the *krater*. Wine was not drunk straight (except by barbarians), and this very large container was used to mix it with water. After mixing, the entire group drank wine from this same source, so the word symposium, literally "a drinking together," was applied to the gathering.

AgPicBk 26 (2005); *Hesperia* Suppl. 46 (2011).

CASES 38–39. OBJECTS FROM A WELL

Cases 38 and 39 display a small selection from the contents of a well near the southeast corner of the Agora. The well had gone out of use and was filled with a mass of debris around the year 400 B.C. On the bottom shelf of Case 38 are typical drinking vessels of the period: *skyphoi* and two-handled and one-handled mugs. Here too are powder boxes and pitchers. On the shelf above rest terracotta figurines, a small bone Herm, a terracotta copy of the lion-head terminal of a bracelet, and an ivory stylus for writing on wax. A particularly noteworthy object from this well is a bronze measure (Fig. 86; no. 12; B 1082), cylindrical in shape and inscribed "official property of the people of Athens"; it holds about 0.111 liter (3.75 oz.), probably an ancient *hemikotylion* (half a *kotyle*—compare with the terracotta measures in Case 68, pp. 146–147).

Case 39 displays characteristic trefoil-mouthed water pitchers (*choes*), some wheelmade and black-glossed, others handshaped and unglossed. One of these unglossed pitchers (Fig. 102; bottom shelf, no. 2; P 23900) bears a scene related to ancient comedy, painted in pastel-like pigments of various colors (white, black, pink, green). This is just one of a group of four. These Athenian pitchers are important documents for the history of the theater, and anticipate the *phlyax* vases of South Italy.

Figure 102. Comic scene on a pitcher, ca. 400 B.C., photograph and watercolor

Figure 103. Red-figure chous *with tripod and Nikai, ca. 410–400 B.C.*

Among the red-figure vases, a pitcher (*chous*) at the top of Case 39 (no. 3; P23877) shows a child among his playthings. This *chous* is of the type carried by children at the "Festival of Pitchers" during the *Anthesteria*. Two other pitchers of similar shape have scenes relating to victories: on one a boy leading a horse holds a victor's wreath in his hand (no. 2; P 23850); on the other a prize tripod is flanked to right and left by Nikai (Fig. 103; P 23896, on long-term loan).

At the bottom of the case are terracotta lamps, loomweights, and a whetstone.

Debris from a well: H. A. Thompson, *Hesperia* 25 (1956), pp. 57–61. **Pitchers with comic scenes**: M. Crosby, *Hesperia* 24 (1955), pp. 76–84; T. B. L. Webster, *Hesperia* 29 (1960), p. 261–263; A. D. Trendall, *Phlyax Vases* (London, 1967, 2nd edition), pp. 23–24; A. D. Trendall and T. B. L. Webster, *Illustrations of Greek Drama* (London, 1971), p. 120; *Agora XII* (1970), p. 205; A. Pickard-Cambridge, *The Dramatic Festivals of Athens* (Oxford, 1988, 2nd edition), pp. 212–213; J. K. Papadopoulos et al. (2007) in *The Art of Antiquity* (Athens, 2007), pp. 169–171.

CASES 60–64, 40–42. HOUSEHOLD POTTERY, COOKING UTENSILS AND DEVICES

The remainder of the cases in this section afford a very good picture of the kitchen and tableware used in an Athenian household of the Classical period. In Case 64, on the left side of the gallery, are displayed some of the most common shapes of tableware. All are covered with the black gloss that maintained its shiny quality throughout the 6th, 5th, and 4th centuries B.C. Most prominent are the vessels for holding and drinking wine. At the top left (no. 1; P 16453) is a wine pitcher (*chous*), glossed to prevent seepage; the garland painted on the shoulder of the jug reminds one of the common uses of garlands at Greek symposia. Below, in the back row (nos. 3–5), are deep, two-handled drinking cups (*skyphoi*) of a type borrowed by the Athenians from Corinth. The shape was popular through the 6th and 5th centuries. In front of them (nos. 9–11) are stemless drinking cups that enjoyed long-lived popularity from the 7th into the 4th century B.C. because they were more practical than their high-stemmed, figured contemporaries. Closer examination shows that some of the black vases are decorated with geometric and floral designs that were stamped or incised before the clay had hardened.

A *kantharos* of the second half of the 5th century is displayed on the top shelf, left (no. 2; P 21877). The plainer specimens to the right (nos. 3, 4, 6) illustrate the most common type of drinking cup in the 4th and early 3rd centuries B.C.

Case 63 holds three utilitarian vessels. The large spherical jug (no. 2; P 20786) still retained a cork in its mouth when found. Dating from ca. 480 B.C., this is the earliest known cork stopper. The jug had been lowered into a well to keep its contents cool. The two-handled basin (*lekane*) behind (no. 1), fully glossed inside and banded outside, served a great variety of household needs. The mushroom jug (no. 3), named for its shape, is a pouring vessel with two handles close together rather than one.

Toward the upper left of Case 62 (nos. 1–3) are three examples of wine coolers (*psykteres*), their bodies tapered so that they could be set into bowls of cold water. Below is a chamberpot (*amis*) (no. 1; P 2352). Near it are two one-handlers (nos. 6 and 8), the most common bowl in this period for table use. On the right of the shelf are a number of informal documents on potsherds: messages, lists, the alphabet, etc. The most numerous category records an owner's name.

The cases at the end of the room (both right and left) move from the table into the kitchen. The equipment comprises a wide range of devices for cooking, all made of a coarse, brown, fire-resistant clay, without paint or decoration of any sort. The top shelf of Case 61 presents the principal types of brazier that were popular in the Classical period. They were designed to hold round-bottomed cooking pots, as illustrated by no. 3, more examples of which are across the gallery in Case 41. On the shelf below (no. 3; P 4869) and next to it in Case 60 (no. 2; P 21956) are two braziers consisting each of a shallow round basin with broad flat rim supported on a low stand. These were evidently designed for grilling with a slow fire of charcoal. The second brazier has long lugs on its rim to support spits for making the equivalent of the modern shishkebab or souvlaki. The bell-shaped devices with them may also have served as portable ovens in which the dough was set beneath and the coals heaped around. A grill is also displayed at the bottom of Case 61 (no. 2).

Cross to Case 42, which displays a second grill (no. 2). In Case 41, on the bottom shelf among the quintessential cooking pots, is an inscribed kitchen inventory (no. 3; P 10810). Case 40 displays two frying pans on the bottom shelf (nos. 2 and 3). Above the pans are a strainer (no. 3) and examples of two of the types of large vessel most commonly used for handling water: a jar with two handles through which a rope could be run for drawing water from the well (a *kados*; no. 2), and a three-handled jar (*hydria*) for carrying the water from well to house (no. 1). These water vessels, made of a micaceous brown clay with extremely thin walls that added little to the burden of the carrier, continued to be shaped by hand long after most other vases were regularly turned on the wheel.

Household pottery: *AgPicBk* 1 (1959); B. A. Sparkes, *JHS* 82 (1962) 121–137; *Agora* XII (1970); *Agora* XXXIII (2006). **Graffiti**: *AgPicBk* 14 (1974; reprinted 1988); *Agora* XXI (1976).

Figure 104. Athenian coins with Athena and owl: (left pair) silver, 5th century B.C.; (right pair) bronze, 2nd century B.C.

CASE 5. COINS

Before continuing onward to the cases of material from the Hellenistic period, stop at the central case displaying some of the 75,000 identifiable coins found in the Agora excavations. The exhibit at the front of the case represents briefly the history of Athenian coinage from its beginnings in the first half of the 6th century B.C. to its conclusion at the time of the Herulian sack of A.D. 267 (Fig. 104). The bronze pieces of the 3rd and 2nd centuries B.C. might have been made on site at the Mint ❻❶. At the back of the case, set in a vertical display so that both sides of the coins are visible, are foreign coins of all periods: specimens of coins minted in other Greek cities, a series of Roman coins beginning in the time of Sulla, and a small sampling of the coinage of the Byzantine empire, of the Frankish occupiers, of the Venetians, and of the Turks, who dominated Athens in turn.

The great majority of coins in the collection are of bronze and of small denominations; the silver coins number almost 500 pieces. Also included (Fig. 105; viewable at the back of the case) are a 5th-century B.C. Kyzikene stater of electrum (an alloy of gold and silver; no. 1) and gold coins from different periods: a Persian daric (no. 2: 465–425 B.C.), a posthumous stater of Alexander the Great struck at Sardis ca. 321 B.C. (no. 3), a Late Roman gold coin of Arcadius (no. 47, row 6), a Venetian ducat (no. 75, row 10: A.D. 1694–1700), three Turkish pieces (no. 88, row 11: A.D. 1574; nos. 93 and 94, bottom row: early 1800s), and a 20-franc piece of Napoleon III (center of row 11: A.D. 1854).

Agora II (1954); *Agora* IX (1962); *AgPicBk* 15 (1975); *AgPicBk* 18 (1978); *Agora* XXVI (1993).

Figure 105. (a) Electrum stater from Kyzikos; (b) gold Persian daric; (c) gold stater of Alexander the Great; (d) gold solidus of Arcadius; (e) gold Venetian ducat; (f) gold Ottoman coin; and (g) gold coin of Napoleon, obverse (left) and reverse (right).

HELLENISTIC (323–86 B.C.), ROMAN (86 B.C.–6TH CENTURY A.D), AND BYZANTINE (10TH–12TH CENTURIES A.D.) PERIODS

The devastation of the war with Sparta and the rise of Macedon under Philip and Alexander led to an Athens with much less political power. However, the patronage of Hellenistic rulers, such as the building of the Stoa of Attalos by Attalos II, king of Pergamon (159–138 B.C.), ensured that the city never lost its cultural influence. The long period between the death of Alexander the Great (323 B.C.) and the siege of Athens by Sulla (86 B.C.) is represented in the museum chiefly by pottery and terracotta figurines.

Although the Agora in the period immediately after the Sullan destruction was encroached upon by private industry, there was a revitalization under Augustus (e.g., the gift of the Odeion of Agrippa). The Roman period saw the continued production of Neo-Attic sculpture begun in the Hellenistic period, and copies were made of the best sculpture from the Archaic and Classical periods. Some examples of these have already been viewed in the colonnade and on the upper floor.

The Herulian invasion of A.D. 267 changed the shape of the city and the Agora through widespread destruction and a shift in the city walls that left the Agora outside them. Nevertheless, Athens held on to its reputation as a center of philosophy, and many of the objects in the museum derive from large villas of the 4th century built on the edge of the old civic center, some of which probably served as philosophical schools.

The final case of the museum displays a few pieces of pottery from the small but substantial residential district that the Agora became during the Byzantine period; these objects date chiefly to the 10th–12th centuries.

Hellenistic: *AgPicBk* 2 (1959; reprinted 1992); J. McK. Camp II, *The Athenian Agora* (London, 1986), pp. 153–180. **Roman–Byzantine**: *AgPicBk* 7 (1961); *Agora* XX (1971); *Agora* XIV (1972), pp. 204–219; J. McK. Camp II, *The Athenian Agora* (London, 1986), pp. 181–214; *Agora* XXIV (1988).

> ⚡ The Hellenistic and Roman material is displayed beyond the pottery cases. Begin with the sculpture on the left side of the gallery.

CASE 59. SCULPTURE AND COPIES OF FAMOUS STATUES

The excavations have yielded many of the simplified miniature copies of popular old statues that were created by Athenian sculptors in the Hellenistic and Roman period. They were intended for the adornment of private houses. The miniature Aphrodite in the center of the top shelf (S 1192: ca. 150–86 B.C.), on whose right shoulder Eros once perched, is of the same type as a colossal statue that now stands in the colonnade of the Stoa (S 378, p. 38). Note the ancient paint. The weary Herakles to the right (S 1241: Roman) references an original of the 4th century B.C., probably by Lysippos. The type is best known from a colossal copy, the "Herakles Farnese" now in Naples, which is signed by an Athenian sculptor, Glykon. On the shelf below (no. 3), the little image of the triple Hekate (S 852: 1st–2nd century A.D.), goddess of crossroads and of entrances, echoes remotely a famous work of Alkamenes on the Acropolis.

Displayed on the left side of the case are two statuettes inspired by cult images in the sanctuaries of the Agora. Above, the heavily draped Apollo with kithara (S 877: uncertain date) is a copy at 1/10 scale of Euphranor's statue of Apollo Patroos, which now stands in the colonnade (S 2154, p. 33). Below, in a little shrine (Fig. 106; S 922: late 4th century B.C.), sits the Mother of the Gods with a *phiale* (an offering dish), *tympanum* (a handheld drum), lion, and attendants, much as she must have appeared in the Metron ⓮.

Figure 106. Miniature copy of the statue of the Mother of the Gods, the original of which stood in the Metroon

The multifigured relief at the center of the bottom shelf of Case 59 is an original of the late 4th century B.C. (no. 2; S 1251). It shows a family of worshippers approaching a group of Eleusinian divinities: Demeter seated, Persephone standing, and Eubouleus (or, less likely, Iakhos) with the infant Wealth (Ploutos) on his arm.

General: *AgPicBk* 27 (2006), figs. 39, 41, 44, 50, 51. **Aphrodite**: T. L. Shear, *Hesperia* 10 (1941), p. 5; A. Stewart, *Hesperia* 81 (2012), pp. 289–292, 297–298, 326–327. **Herakles**: H A. Thompson, *Hesperia* 17 (1948), p. 180. **Hekate**: *Agora* XI (1965), p. 103, no. 147. **Apollo**: *Agora* XIV (1972), p. 139. **Mother**: *Agora* XIV (1972), p. 31; M. Munn, *The Mother of the Gods, Athens, and the Tyranny of Asia* (Berkeley, 2006), pp. 62–64. **Eleusinian deities**: H. A. Thompson, *Hesperia* 17 (1948), pp. 177–178; *Agora* XXXI (1998), pp. 218–219, no. 7.

CASES 56–58. ROMAN SCULPTURE

A number of particularly fine portrait busts and heads of the 1st B.C.–early 1st A.D. are displayed in Case 58. Note especially the head of an Egyptian priest dating from the 1st century B.C. (no. 1; S 333); his profession is shown by the shaven skull and headband. In the center is the head of a young woman whose distinctive coiffure points to the time of Tiberius (no. 2; S 1631: A.D. 14–37). There is also a strikingly beautiful bust of a young man of the Julio-Claudian period (early 1st century A.D.), perhaps a member of the imperial family (no. 3; S 356).

Figure 107. Roman portrait of a man found in the Library of Pantainos, ca. 100 A.D.

In Case 57 is a youthful satyr holding a goat at his left side; in his right hand is a panpipe (photo p. 11, top center; S 221). The porcelain finish of the flesh, contrasting effectively with the rough surface of hair and hide, is characteristic of the Antonine period (mid-2nd century A.D.). Note the traces of ancient paint on the hair.

The three final portraits in Case 56 (S 1182, S 1299, S 2468) should all date to the early 2nd century A.D. The one on the far right may represent Pantainos, the dedicator of the library **48**, if its discovery in that building is significant (Fig. 107).

Portraits: *Agora* I (1953); *AgPicBk* 5 (1960). **Satyr**: T. L. Shear, *Hesperia* 2 (1933), pp. 536–541.

CASE 6. IVORY STATUETTE OF APOLLO LYKEIOS; IVORY, GOLD, AND GLASS

The last piece of sculpture is found on the front side of the central case. The foot-high ivory statuette of the resting Apollo (BI 236) once held a bow or lyre in his outstretched left hand. This is a miniature replica, made in the 2nd or 3rd century A.D., of a work of the 4th century B.C. that stood in the Lyceum gymnasium in Athens. The common attribution of the original to Praxiteles is not certain, but its fame is attested by the number of extant replicas. The ivory was found shattered into more than 200 fragments in a well (Fig. 108).

On the opposite side of the case is a collection of ivory, bone, glass, and gold objects. The semicircular bone plaque (no. 6; BI 288) once adorned the end of a small casket of the 4th or 5th century A.D. In the middle stands a voluminously draped figure holding a pair of spears in the left hand and a plumed helmet in the right. In the field to the left are two bundles, to the right an *amphora*. The identification of the figure is difficult. The massive ivory crossbar from a sword hilt (no. 5; BI 457) is a rare and noteworthy object. Also displayed here are several glass vessels and pieces of gold jewelry of the Roman period.

Ivory Apollo: T. L. Shear, *Hesperia* 6 (1937), pp. 349–351; *AgPicBk* 3 (1959), fig. 60; A. Paterakis, *OSGP* 5 (1997), pp. 75–79; C. Lawton in *The Art of Antiquity* (Athens, 2007), pp. 228–229. **Bone plaque**: T. L. Shear, *Hesperia* 6 (1937), pp. 380–381. **Glass**: *Agora* XXXIV (2009).

CASES 43–46. POTTERY OF THE HELLENISTIC PERIOD

Return to the right side of the gallery to examine the pottery. By the last quarter of the 4th century B.C. the old red-figure style had died a natural death. It was succeeded by various other techniques for the decoration of vases. One innovation was the use of thinned clay and white paint for the application of floral and geometric designs: the so-called West Slope style, named from the discovery of much of this ware on the west slope of the Acropolis in the 1890s. In this period molds too were commonly used to achieve an imitation of metal vessels with decoration in low relief, especially in the so-called Megarian bowls, once mistakenly believed to have originated in Megara. The old black-figure technique still occurred sporadically, notably on the Panathenaic prize amphoras (Case 34, p. 156). The technical quality of

Figure 108. Ivory statuette of Apollo Lykeios, 2nd–3rd century A.D.: (top) fragments laid out; (bottom) after restoration.

Figure 109. Kantharos *decorated in West Slope technique and inscribed with a* toast, ca. 275 B.C.

the pottery declined after the 4th century, in part because metal vessels came to be more commonly used by those who could afford them while the less affluent were satisfied by imitations of metal in clay.

Case 43 exhibits several good specimens of the West Slope technique. The tall-stemmed drinking cup (*kantharos*) at the end of the top shelf (Fig. 109; no. 6; P 5811) is inscribed with a toast to friendship (*philia*). The enormous *kantharos* on the bottom shelf (no. 1; P 6878) bears a dedication by Menokles to Dionysos and Artemis. On the better-preserved side is a hunting scene with a little shrine of Artemis, goddess of the hunt, in the middle (photo p. 11, bottom left). On the bottom shelf are displayed assorted pieces of gold jewelry, almost all recovered from the well near the northwest crossroads **㉗** (see the *Agora Site Guide,* p. 86). Note especially the earrings in the form of winged Erotes.

On the top shelf of Case 44 is an imitation of a "Hadra *hydria,*" a type used as ash urns in the Hadra cemetery of Alexandria (no. 1; P 6313). This type of vessel is rarely found in Athens. The bottom shelf of this case has several examples of the *lagynos,* a type of wine jug with

Figure 110. Moldmade bowl with lotus petals, with detail of rosette medallion on the bottom, ca. 225–200 B.C.

a tall slender neck and either a globular or an angular body, popular in the Hellenistic period. Those with a creamy white wash were imported to Athens, probably from Asia Minor.

The neighboring cases contain a medley of characteristic products of Hellenistic craftsmanship. The manufacture of "Megarian bowls," an active industry in Athens from the last quarter of the 3rd to the middle of the 1st century B.C., is illustrated by molds and by stamps for the making of molds on the bottom shelf of Case 45 (nos. 4–9). Some of the earlier bowls with purely floral decoration in very delicate, crisp relief must resemble metal prototypes (Fig. 110; top shelf, no. 3; P 19908). These are followed by a group with figured decoration, miscellaneous but chiefly idyllic in its themes (no. 2). About the middle of the 2nd century B.C. a calyx-like scheme of long petals came into favor and persisted to the end (no. 4). As seen in Case 47 (pp. 178–180), terracotta lamps of the period often share the relief decoration of the "Megarian bowls."

In this case also, at the bottom, is a moldmade wine-mixing bowl (*krater*) of gray clay from Asia Minor (no. 2; P 3155). Note that the figures on the neck (satyrs, maenads, etc., appropriate to the festive use of the bowl) were molded separately and applied. Both the *krater* itself and the handles are clearly derived from metal originals.

The spindle-shaped unguent bottles of gray clay in Case 46 (bottom shelf, nos. 7 and 9) are found on virtually all sites of the Hellenistic period in the eastern Mediterranean. The bottles and their contents must have originated in some common center, but the characteristic

The flying Victory (Nike) hanging on the back of the case is a creation of the 3rd century B.C. Note the cuttings for wings in the shoulders (no. 2; T 2309). She is flanked by Erotes, also in flight.

Terracottas: D. B. Thompson, *Hesperia* 2 (1933), pp. 184–194; *AgPicBk* 3 (1951); *Agora* VI (1961); H. A. Thompson, D. B. Thompson, and S. I. Rotroff, *Hellenistic Pottery and Terracottas* (Princeton, 1987). **Impressions from ancient metal work**: D. B. Thompson, *Hesperia* 8 (1938), pp. 285–316; *Hesperia* Suppl. 8 (1949), pp. 365–372; *Hesperia* 38 (1969), pp. 242–251; E. R. Williams, *Hesperia* 45 (1976), pp. 41–66. **Theatral figures**: T. B. L. Webster, *Hesperia* 29 (1960), pp. 254–284.

CASES 48–49. VARIOUS OBJECTS OF THE ROMAN PERIOD

The neighboring cases to the left are more miscellaneous. The period extends from the 1st century B.C. to the 5th century A.D. The figures of the Early Roman period, Aphrodite and Eros in both bronze and terracotta on the top shelf of Case 48 (nos. 3–6), are little more than miniature echoes of famous old sculptural types. More interesting for the history of art are the crude yet vigorous terracottas of the 4th and 5th centuries A.D. on the bottom shelf. Here the coroplast is working more independently. He is no longer concerned with delicacy of modeling, but depends largely on incision and paint. Note especially the bearded head in the lower right (no. 16; T 3055), the toy dog in the center (no. 6; T 1510), and the seated woman suckling a child in the back right (no. 12; T 511), a type that stands midway between the Isis and Horus of Egypt and the Virgin and Child of Christian art. In the Late Roman period the coroplast devoted much of his talent to the making of hand-modeled lamps and of children's playthings, both well represented here.

The "baroque" satyr's head in the middle (no. 10; BI 752) is a good example of ivory carving of the 2nd century A.D.; the ivory must have adorned a piece of furniture. To the left are some gaming pieces (nos. 8 and 9): besides the dice there are some knucklebones of sheep (*astragaloi*), which were favorite playthings of Greek children.

On the back wall above are hung two life-size terracotta masks of the 3rd century A.D. (nos. 1 and 2; T 1818, T 478). They must be patterned closely on the masks, presumably of lighter and tougher material, used in the theater. No. 1 is taken from a figure of tragic pantomime; the other represents the "leading slave," a stock figure in Roman comedy.

The bronze serpent with human head and flowing locks on the shelf below them is one of the few known representations of Glykon, a reincarnation of the god Asklepios that was brought about by a magician in Anatolia in the 2nd century A.D. (no. 8; B 253).

Case 49 assembles a few characteristic products of craftsmanship of the Roman period, both local and imported. In the Roman period, in contrast with earlier times, a considerable proportion of the fine pottery used in Athens was imported. This was due in part to losses suffered by the potters in the siege of Athens by Sulla in 86 B.C. At the upper right of the case is a bowl of the latter part of the 1st century B.C. made at Arretium in north Italy (no. 4; P 17219). Below, the large plate of thin red fabric with figures in low relief is also imported, perhaps from North Africa. It dates to the 3rd century A.D. Note also on this shelf (no. 6;

Figure 112. Roman relief jug, 1st century A.D.

P 19267) a terracotta bowl with the head of the Emperor Augustus in high relief on its floor (photo p. 11, bottom center; no. 6; P19267).

Christian symbols first come into common use in Athens in the 5th century A.D. Several are shown here: a water pitcher with a Christian monogram and the incised inscription "of the Virgin" (no. 2; P 25133), a fragment from the floor of a red ware plate with the head of an unknown martyr bearing his cross (no. 8; P 197), and a bronze lamp with a cross (no. 10; B 579).

On the top shelf are pitchers of the 3rd century A.D. molded in the shape of boys' heads (P 10004, P 11939), to be compared with the contemporary marble portraits in Case 56 across the gallery (p. 173). There is also a wine jug of the 1st century A.D. decorated in relief with applied clay (no. 3; P 10714). On the bottom shelf is a similar relief jug, though created through the use of moulds (Fig. 112; no. 1; P 17877, on long-term loan).

Roman pottery and figurines: *Agora* V (1959); *AgPicBk* 3 (1959); *Agora* VI (1961); *Agora* XXXII (2008). **Portrait medallions**: *AgPicBk* 5, figs. 3–6.

CASE 50. LAMPS

From the approximately 6,000 terracotta lamps found in the excavations, enough have been displayed here to illustrate the development of this common household article. The series starts at the upper left (no. 1) with a hand-shaped open saucer of a type borrowed by the Greeks from the Near East along with many other things in the 7th century B.C. The form was gradually improved and

Figure 113. Black-gloss lamp, ca. 480–415 B.C.

made more practical: the rim was bent in to prevent spilling, a nozzle was devised to hold the wick more firmly, a handle was added, and gloss was applied to make the clay more impervious to oil (Fig. 113; top shelf, no. 4). From the 6th into the 3rd century B.C. lamps were turned on the potter's wheel.

In the Hellenistic period lamps were normally made with a pair of molds, one for the upper and one for the lower part (one such mold is shown here, bottom shelf, no. 4). The new technique speeded production and permitted the addition of some hand-modeled ornamentation similar to that found on the contemporary "Megarian bowls."

In the 1st century B.C. the top of the lamp (discus) began to be treated as a field for a circular relief in which were represented a great variety of themes. In the Athenian shops technical skill reached its climax in the 2nd and 3rd centuries A.D. At the left (no. 13; L 4251) is a lamp discus of the 3rd century A.D. illustrating the story of Hero and Leander: Leander, vigorously swimming the Hellespont, is guided shoreward by the lamp that Hero holds out from a window high in her tower. Thereafter invention failed; molds were made from lamps and lamps from molds with the same theme until it became a coarse caricature of the original. By the 6th century Athenian lamps were utterly degenerate both artistically and technically. When the industry revived in the Byzantine period the cycle began afresh with an open saucer form (no. 21).

Figure 114. Lamp with discus depicting St. Peter, 5th century A.D.

Christian themes can be seen on some of the later lamps. On no. 18 (Fig. 114; L 4754) St. Peter is shown at full length with his cross of martyrdom, and a fragment from the discus of a lamp (no. 17; L 1153) bears the head of St. Paul.

In all periods the fuel used was vegetable oil, chiefly olive. It was fed through a fabric wick like that put in place in one of the lamps on the bottom shelf (no. 5). Such lamps will burn for one to two hours giving as much light as a candle.

Agora IV (1958; reprinted 1966); *Agora* VI (1961); *AgPicBk* 9 (1963).

CASES 51–54. OBJECTS FROM A WELL

The cases at the north end of the gallery display a small selection of the objects recovered from a single well on the north slope of the Areopagus. At 35 m (115 ft), this well happens to be one of the deepest, but it is typical in the wide variety of objects that had been dropped or thrown into it. The stratified deposit runs from the 1st into the 6th century A.D. After a break marking the Dark Age in Athens, the record resumes for a short period in the 10th century (Fig. 115; a chart detailing the different strata can be seen on the wall of Case 53). A few characteristic pieces have been laid out by century starting with the earliest in Case 51. One can observe the changes in fashion in tableware through the ages. The several complete lamps attest to many night journeys to the well.

The most numerous finds are the vessels for water. They include many pitchers for carrying water from the well into the house. The medium-sized jars with basket handles will have been used for drawing water on the end of rope (Case 51, bottom shelf, no. 2).

Also in Case 51 is a pair of dice (bottom, no. 7). Other possible playthings, attractive seashells, are displayed in the following case (Case 52, no. 9). Next to them, the walnuts and peach stones (no. 10) are interesting indications of diet.

At the top of Case 53 is a terracotta figurine (no. 5). On the same shelf is another basket-handled jar (no. 1), one of the latest examples of the type. Here too is a water carrier not made of pottery: a lead pail of the 4th century A.D. (no. 9; IL 563). Two wooden buckets of the same period, made of staves, were also found, but are not on display (W 6, W 14).

Agora V (1959), pp. 82–120, Group M; *Agora* XXXII (2008).

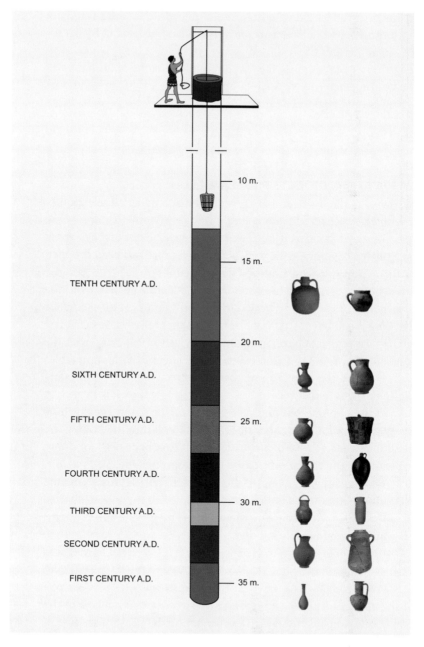

Figure 115. Drawing of the stratified filling of a well in use from the 1st to the 10th century A.D.

WELLS

Over 450 ancient wells (Fig. 116) have been excavated in the area of the Agora. Wells were an essential component of the water supply of the ancient city and are now a valuable resource for archaeologists. In order to collect fresh ground water for daily use, a deep shaft was cut into the ground through the soft bedrock. Occasionally this shaft was lined with small stones to combat possible collapse. Foot- and handholds were carved into the sides, which made periodic cleaning easier. At the end of the 5th century B.C., a new technology was introduced: wells began to be lined with large terracotta tiles backed by stones. This became the standard form of construction by the Hellenistic period, though at that time cisterns—large underground containers with a waterproof lining—surpassed wells as the preferred water receptacle. Over the opening of the well was a cover to prevent objects, people, or animals from falling in. A cover might be as simple as a large, reused jar, or the well could be topped by a cylindrical puteal like the ones at the north end of the museum terrace (Fig. 19, p. 29). Typically water was drawn by means of a rope and a jar, but the use of a winch is not unknown. The jars occasionally slipped and ended up at the bottom of the well where they created an archaeological deposit, the period of use fill.

Because wells were set into the ground, they are more likely to survive when above-ground structures do not. The evidence for the Neolithic occupants of the area of the Agora derives almost entirely from wells (Case 81, p. 103). Most of the Agora wells are associated with houses; tracing their locations over time allows us to map the shifting neighborhoods of Athens and the movable boundaries of public and private space. This exercise is especially useful on the east side of the Agora square where no standing architecture earlier than the Hellenistic period is preserved. The contents of these wells, as seen in many of the gallery cases, provide other kinds of information. A well that was used over a long period of time contains stratigraphic data useful for producing a relative chronology of objects, especially pottery. For

Figure 116. The author emerges from a well

example, the selection of objects from a well 35 m deep covers a span of several centuries, showing the change in forms over time (Fig. 115; Cases 51–54, pp. 183–184). When a well went out of use, it was filled up with debris, and this ancient garbage can reveal what activities were taking place nearby. The wells that were closed after the Persian invasion of Athens (480 B.C.) contain material from the buildings that used them. In some cases, it is possible to reconstruct a single household's kitchen and dining equipment at a specific point in time, and a few wells can be connected to shops that sold pottery.

AgPicBk 11 (1968); *Hesperia* Suppl. 46 (2011).

CASE 55. GLAZED POTTERY

This case contains a selection of the finer pottery found in the ruins of the houses that overlay much of the Agora from the 10th to the 12th centuries A.D. Most of these wares were imported into Athens.

Many of the vessels, dating from the 11th and 12th centuries A.D., are decorated in the *sgraffito* technique. A dark-colored clay was overlaid with a thick slip of creamy white. When the slip became firm the designs were incised through it into the dark clay, and parts of the background were scraped clear of slip so as to make the design stand out in light against dark. The whole of the decorated surface was then overlaid with a protecting coat of thin, almost colorless glaze. Birds and animals appear commonly in the medallions that are surrounded by elaborate geometric ornament and occasionally by imitations of Arabic writing (pseudo-Kufic), e.g., no. 2 on the wall (P 5026). In a coarser and slightly earlier ware, illustrated by the large bowl on the bottom right (no. 10; P 9552), the design, instead of being incised, has been painted in matte colors (green and black) over a light slip and then protected as before by a transparent glaze. The top shelf displays two glazed chafing dishes, each with a small compartment for a charcoal fire to keep food warm (nos. 1 and 5; P 3075, P 10147).

The fragments of *sgraffito* plates and bowls on the bottom of the case illustrate some of the exploits of Digenis Akritas, the Herakles of the Byzantine period. Note especially the middle piece (no. 7; P 8623) in which Digenis, in keeping with the songs of the epic cycle, is killing a dragon with five arrows (photo p. 11, bottom right).

M. A. Frantz, *Hesperia* 7 (1938), pp. 429–467; M. A. Franz, *Hesperia* 10 (1941), pp. 9–13 (Akritas); *AgPicBk* 7 (1961); C. MacKay in *The Art of Antiquity* (Athens, 2007), pp. 276–285.

ABBREVIATIONS

AA	*Archäologischer Anzeiger*
AgPicBk	*Athenian Agora Picture Books*
AJA	*American Journal of Archaeology*
AJP	*American Journal of Philology*
AM	*Mitteilungen des Deutschen Archäologischen Instituts, Athenische Abteilung*
AntP	*Antike Plastik*
ArchEph	*Αρχαιολογική Εφημερίς*
Chiron	*Chiron. Mitteilungen der Kommission für alte Geschichte und Epigraphik des Deutschen Archäologischen Instituts*
DOP	*Dumbarton Oaks Papers*
Hesperia	*Hesperia. The Journal of the American School of Classical Studies at Athens*
Historia	*Historia. Zeitschrift für alte Geschichte*
HSCP	*Harvard Studies in Classical Philology*
JdI	*Jahrbuch des Deutschen Archäologischen Instituts*
JHS	*Journal of Hellenic Studies*
JWalt	*Journal of the Walters Art Gallery*
OJA	*Oxford Journal of Archaeology*
OpAth	*Opuscula Atheniensia*
OpRom	*Opuscula Romana*
OSGP	*Objects Specialty Group Postprints*
Phoenix	*Phoenix. The Classical Association of Canada*
RÉA	*Revue des études anciennes*
RendLinc	*Atti dell'Accademia nazionale dei Lincei. Rendiconti*
RM	*Mitteilungen des Deutschen Archäologischen Instituts, Römische Abteilung*
ZPE	*Zeitschrift für Papyrologie und Epigraphik*

List of
Publications

LIST OF PUBLICATIONS CONCERNING THE ATHENIAN AGORA PUBLISHED BY THE AMERICAN SCHOOL OF CLASSICAL STUDIES AT ATHENS

THE ATHENIAN AGORA: RESULTS OF EXCAVATIONS CONDUCTED BY THE AMERICAN SCHOOL OF CLASSICAL STUDIES AT ATHENS

A series of scholarly monographs on the final results of the excavations.

I E. B. Harrison, *Portrait Sculpture* (1953).

II M. Thompson, *Coins: From the Roman through the Venetian Period* (1954).

III R. E. Wycherley, *Literary and Epigraphical Testimonia* (1957; reprinted 1973).

IV R. H. Howland, *Greek Lamps and Their Survivals* (1958; reprinted 1966).

V H. S. Robinson, *Pottery of the Roman Period: Chronology* (1959).

VI C. Grandjouan, *Terracottas and Plastic Lamps of the Roman Period* (1961).

VII J. Perlzweig, *Lamps of the Roman Period: First to Seventh Century after Christ* (1961; reprinted 1971).

VIII E. T. H. Brann, *Late Geometric and Protoattic Pottery: Mid-8th to Late 7th Century B.C.* (1962; reprinted 1971).

IX G. C. Miles, *The Islamic Coins* (1962).

X M. Lang and M. Crosby, *Weights, Measures, and Tokens* (1964).

XI E. B. Harrison, *Archaic and Archaistic Sculpture* (1965).

XII B. A. Sparkes and L. Talcott, *Black and Plain Pottery of the 6th, 5th, and 4th Centuries B.C.* (1970).

XIII S. A. Immerwahr, *The Neolithic and Bronze Ages* (1971).

XIV H. A. Thompson and R. E. Wycherley, *The Agora of Athens: The History, Shape, and Uses of an Ancient City Center* (1972).

XV B. D. Meritt and J. S. Traill, *Inscriptions: The Athenian Councillors* (1974).

XVI A. G. Woodhead, *Inscriptions: The Decrees* (1997).

XVII D. W. Bradeen, *Inscriptions: The Funerary Monuments* (1974).

XVIII D. J. Geagan, *Inscriptions: The Dedicatory Monuments* (2011).

XIX   G. V. Lalonde, M. K. Langdon, and M. B. Walbank, *Inscriptions: Horoi, Poletai Records, and Leases of Public Lands* (1991).

XX   A. Frantz, *The Church of the Holy Apostles* (1971).

XXI   M. Lang, *Graffiti and Dipinti* (1976).

XXII   S. I. Rotroff, *Hellenistic Pottery: Athenian and Imported Moldmade Bowls* (1982).

XXIII   M. B. Moore and M. Z. P. Philippides, *Attic Black-Figured Pottery* (1986).

XXIV   A. Frantz, *Late Antiquity: A.D. 267–700* (1988).

XXV   M. Lang, *Ostraka* (1990).

XXVI   J. H. Kroll, with A. S. Walker, *The Greek Coins* (1993).

XXVII   R. F. Townsend, *The East Side of the Agora: The Remains beneath the Stoa of Attalos* (1995).

XXVIII   A. L. Boegehold et al., *The Lawcourts at Athens: Sites, Buildings, Equipment, Procedure, and Testimonia* (1995).

XXIX   S. I. Rotroff, *Hellenistic Pottery: Athenian and Imported Wheelmade Table Ware and Related Material* (1997).

XXX   M. B. Moore, *Attic Red-Figured and White-Ground Pottery* (1997).

XXXI   M. M. Miles, *The City Eleusinion* (1998).

XXXII   J. W. Hayes, *Roman Pottery: Fine-Ware Imports* (2008).

XXXIII   S. I. Rotroff, *Hellenistic Pottery: The Plain Wares* (2006).

XXXIV   G. D. Weinberg and E. M. Stern, *Vessel Glass* (2009).

XXXV   J. B. Grossman, *Funerary Sculpture* (2013).

ATHENIAN AGORA PICTURE BOOKS

Short thematic surveys (32–50 pages) with numerous illustrations and a brief text. Those marked with an * are also available in Modern Greek.

1.   B. A. Sparkes and L. Talcott, *Pots and Pans of Classical Athens* (1959).

2.   H. A. Thompson, *The Stoa of Attalos II in Athens* (1959; reprinted 1992).

3.   D. B. Thompson, *Miniature Sculpture from the Athenian Agora* (1959).

4.* M. Lang, *The Athenian Citizen: Democracy in the Athenian Agora* (revised 2004).

5. E. B. Harrison, *Ancient Portraits from the Athenian Agora* (1960).

6. V. R. Grace, *Amphoras and the Ancient Wine Trade* (revised 1979).

7. A. Frantz, *The Middle Ages in the Athenian Agora* (1961).

8. D. B. Thompson and R. E. Griswold, *Garden Lore of Ancient Athens* (1963).

9. J. Perlzweig, *Lamps from the Athenian Agora* (1963).

10. B. D. Meritt, *Inscriptions from the Athenian Agora* (1966).

11. M. Lang, *Waterworks in the Athenian Agora* (1968).

12. D. B. Thompson, *An Ancient Shopping Center: The Athenian Agora* (revised 1993).

13. S. A. Immerwahr, *Early Burials from the Agora Cemeteries* (1973).

14. M. Lang, *Graffiti in the Athenian Agora* (1974; reprinted 1988).

15. F. S. Kleiner, *Greek and Roman Coins in the Athenian Agora* (1975).

16.* J. McK. Camp II, *The Athenian Agora: A Short Guide* (revised 2003).

17. M. Lang, *Socrates in the Agora* (1978).

18. F. S. Kleiner, *Mediaeval and Modern Coins in the Athenian Agora* (1978).

19. J. McK. Camp II, *Gods and Heroes in the Athenian Agora* (1980).

20. C. C. Mattusch, *Bronzeworkers in the Athenian Agora* (1982).

21. J. McK. Camp II and W. B. Dinsmoor Jr., *Ancient Athenian Building Methods* (1984).

22. R. D. Lamberton and S. I. Rotroff, *Birds of the Athenian Agora* (1985).

23. M. Lang, *Life, Death, and Litigation in the Athenian Agora* (1994).

24. J. McK. Camp II, *Horses and Horsemanship in the Athenian Agora* (1998).

25. J. Neils and S. V. Tracy, *The Games at Athens* (2003).

26. S. I. Rotroff and R. D. Lamberton, *Women in the Athenian Agora* (2006).

27. C. Lawton, *Marbleworkers in the Athenian Agora* (2006).

HESPERIA SUPPLEMENTS

Issued at irregular intervals in the same format as *Hesperia: The Journal of the American School of Classical Studies at Athens*. Volumes concerning Agora material are:

1. S. Dow, *Prytaneis: A Study of the Inscriptions Honoring the Athenian Councillors* (1937).

2. R. S. Young, *Late Geometric Graves and a Seventh-Century Well in the Agora* (1939).

4. H. A. Thompson, *The Tholos of Athens and Its Predecessors* (1940).

5. W. B. Dinsmoor, *Observations on the Hephaisteion* (1941).

8. *Commemorative Studies in Honor of Theodore Leslie Shear* (1949).

9. J. V. A. Fine, *Horoi: Studies in Mortgage, Real Security, and Land Tenure in Ancient Athens* (1951).

12. D. J. Geagan, *The Athenian Constitution after Sulla* (1967).

13. J. H. Oliver, *Marcus Aurelius: Aspects of Civic and Cultural Policy in the East* (1970).

14. J. S. Traill, *The Political Organization of Attica* (1975).

17. T. L. Shear Jr., *Kallias of Sphettos and the Revolt of Athens in 286 B.C.* (1978).

19. *Studies in Attic Epigraphy, History, and Topography Presented to Eugene Vanderpool* (1982).

20. *Studies in Athenian Architecture, Sculpture, and Topography Presented to Homer A. Thompson* (1982).

22. E. J. Walters, *Attic Grave Reliefs That Represent Women in the Dress of Isis* (1988).

23. C. Grandjouan, *Hellenistic Relief Molds from the Athenian Agora* (1989).

25. S. I. Rotroff and J. H. Oakley, *Debris from a Public Dining Place in the Athenian Agora* (1992).

29. R. S. Stroud, *The Athenian Grain-Tax Law of 374/3 B.C.* (1998).

31. J. K. Papadopoulos, *Ceramicus Redivivus: The Early Iron Age Potters' Field in the Area of the Classical Athenian Agora* (2003).

38. M. B. Walbank, *Fragmentary Decrees from the Athenian Agora* (2008).

46. K. M. Lynch, *The Symposium in Context: Pottery from a Late Archaic House near the Athenian Agora* (2011).

47. S. I. Rotroff, *Industrial Religion: The Saucer Pyres of the Athenian Agora* (2013).

OTHER BOOKS

C. A. Mauzy, *Agora Excavations, 1931–2006: A Pictorial History* (2006).

J. K. Papadopoulos et al., *The Art of Antiquity: Piet de Jong and the Athenian Agora* (2007).

INDEX

= ancient literary source

CAPTIONS AND CREDITS

Page 6: Entering the Athenian Agora Museum in the reconstructed Stoa of Attalos

Page 9: A museum visitor reads about the 336 B.C. decree against tyranny

Pages 10–11: Top row, left to right
Neolithic marble figurine of a reclining woman; marble head of an Archaic kore; draped statue of Aphrodite, 4th century B.C.; large triangular tripod base with a maenad advancing right, 3rd century B.C.; statue of a satyr with goat, 2nd century A.D.; statue of a magistrate, 5th century A.D.

Pages 10–11: Bottom row, left to right
Mycenaean kylix with octopus decoration, LH IIIA–B; black-figure skyphos, ca. 500 B.C.; red-figure oinochoe, 5th century B.C; painted kantharos with graffito, figured West Slope ware, 3rd century B.C.; Roman bowl with emblema; Byzantine plate with sgraffito, 12th century A.D.

Pages 12–13: Colonnade of the Stoa of Attalos, watercolor by Piet de Jong

Page 19: A view of the Athenian Agora toward the southeast

Page 78 (Fig. 47): Drawing by C. Link

Page 110 (Fig. 63): Drawing by Graham Houston

Unless otherwise noted, all photographs are courtesy of the Agora Excavations.